TABLE OF CONTENTS

❖ The Original "New Deal:" Impact on North Omaha
❖ North Omaha: Placation and Long-Term Takeover Strategies
❖ Words and Symbols Set the Table
❖ The Fair Deal Urban District: Abra-Kadabra!
❖ Conclusion

What Might Have Been: The Portland, Oregon Example
Conclusion
References

EXECUTIVE SUMMARY

While welfare and social service assistance has always been frowned upon by white decision makers as some kind of "handout," I view the abuse of the Community Development Block Grant programs across this nation in a far more "leech off the government" perspective; in simpler terms, federal grant money is the white man's government cheese. And here's why::

> According to the U.S. Department of Housing and Urban Development: "the Community Development Block Grant (CDBG) program is a flexible program that provides communities [like Lewiston] with resources to address a wide range of unique community development needs." (Gilbert, 2011)

The key word is "flexible" and another term that sums up the way this program has been manhandled by white boys from on high would be "discretion." When you add these two words, you have a carte blanche system that allows mayors and their cronies to spend, spend, spend – and not on the low-income people or areas that the program was designed for. For these cities it's like a big game show and no matter what you do, you win!!!

The key is to meet the basic criteria and if you can do that (with low income and black numbers being manipulated) then you can keep getting money year in and year out without having to show any positive or productive outcomes:

> Beginning in 1974, the CDBG program is one of the longest continuously run programs at HUD. The CDBG program provides annual grants on a formula basis to 1,209 general units of local government and states. Lewiston is one of

those units, as we are an entitlement community. (Gilbert, 2011).

Why did it begin in 1974? Because white folks were afraid of black folks, and because of the civil rights and black power movements, those in power were being bombarded with information that heretofore had been kept out of (by design) the history books. America found out, thanks to the 1960s radicals (black and white) that their country was more fucked up than they thought. So various pacification programs were put in place – and all of them included ways that those in power at the local level could get their "piece of the rock."

The Community Development Block Grant program was one such tactic. In sum,

> The CDBG program provides annual grants to entitled cities, urban communities and states for affordable housing, community development and economic programs primarily for low- and moderate-income persons (Gentile, 2007).

The equation was simple enough: if you had the population size and a poor area (known as a "pocket of poverty") and you promised, in your application, that you would provide for the poor in terms of social services, housing, food, employment and the like, we (meaning the government) will give you (meaning the cities) a Community Development Block Grant – free money. More specifically,

> CDBG allocations are based on complicated formulas that take into account a community's population, poverty level, overcrowding, volume of pre-1940s housing stock and a statistic called "growth lag," which measures how slowly a city has grown relative to other cities (Holeywell, 2012).

The equation backfired as cities got increasingly greedy, and the tendency to perennially ignore the same areas that qualified these cities for the money in the first place. As years passed the cities that were recipients should have been meccas of development and growth; but just look around. Almost every city that has been receiving CDBG funds has a black community that looks the same or worse than it did in the mid-1970s when the money was initially dispersed. And those same cities have downtowns, suburban areas, mega-parks and all types of leisure that they now have because of how they spent that money.

The government really had no oversight. They believed these cities when they submitted their proposals, year after year, lying and claiming that they were making progress and, as examples, documented how much housing they built or renovated (that black people couldn't get into), how many hot meals they served, how many social programs they created. But there was very little that was permanent as far as black people were concerned. We will use Omaha as the prototypical example of the games and gooniness that was an integral part of the *43 years of CDBG money they got – because of black poverty. And when they got it – in excess of $240 million – North Omaha has very little to show for it.*

INTRODUCTION

A cultural nationalist from many years ago once wrote that, "Nationalism demands study. Show me a true nationalist and I'll show you someone who studies" (Karenga, 1967). I never forgot that and I've been studying most of my life – not only when assigned by some teacher who couldn't care less, but because I knew that if black people were going to survive, we had to be informed. The white man used to say that if you wanted to hide something from a nigger, put it in a book. I also never forgot THAT.

I fell in love with North Omaha in 1977 when I arrived there in the summer of that year, supposedly to take a break from my hectic life in the California Bay Area. But when I visited the University of Nebraska at Omaha and saw that it had a Black Studies Department as well as a "major," I transferred my financial aid package and scholarship from the University of California Santa Barbara (where I had been accepted for Fall term 1977) and move to Omaha.

What I saw was a vibrant black community, far more cohesive than the one in Pittsburg or Oakland. I saw black people speaking to and greeting each other. I saw young and old alike walking down the street, and students gathered outside of the Omaha Opportunities and Industrialization during their breaks, numbering in the hundreds. I saw a Black Museum in the heart of the black community, and a militant black state senator who had been just been elected to the Legislature and who was raising hell. All this showed me that this was the place I needed to be.

If I saw it, others who were intelligent also had to see it. The people who lived in North Omaha – the black community – had taken such an incredible situation for granted. With the exception of a few poverty pimps, the grassroots brothers and sisters were working, going to school, taking care of kids and just living their lives.

I enrolled at UNO, declared my major as both Black Studies and Urban Studies, and began studying, with an emphasis on community development and North Omaha. What I began to find, over the years, was a conspiracy that was aimed at bleeding the Northside dry while, at the same time, building and expanding the rest of the city. This brief paper is an outline of how Omaha underdeveloped the state's largest black community, euphemistically known as "the Northside."

I have been writing about black community development and working in the area for over four decades, not only in Omaha but in Milwaukee and Dallas. I have filed injunctions against Omaha for its abuse of Community Development Block Grant funds, filed grievances against the Omaha Public Schools for disparate placement of black kids into Educable Mentally Handicapped classes while hardly any were in the Gifted and Talented sector, and, in general, raised hell and bought attention to why Omaha was segregated and how black people were slowly but surely being disenfranchised.

Although I had reams of newspaper articles, black papers and 200-plus page manuscripts covering almost every sector of black life in the Northside, it was most recently two articles that prompted the writing of this particular manuscript. The first one appeared in the New York Times on December 21,2011 under the headline, "Cities Face Tough Choices as U.S. Slashes Block Grants Program." Written by Michael Cooper, the article was just another "news story" for them, but for me it was confirmation of what I had been warning North Omahans about via radio, television and newspaper for more than two decades. The second article appeared half a year later on the other coast (California). Titled, "Cities face tough choices as federal funding for community programs dries up," the article appeared in the San Gabriel (California) Tribune, and was written by J.D. Velasco, and appeared on May 8, 2012.

In the next section I am going to use the contents of both of these articles as a basis for my analysis of the CDBG program, white leadership attitudes about it, confirmation of my past allegations in regard to Omaha's abuse of it, and all this pertains to the under-development of North Omaha. My observations will also include critiques of the articles themselves.

CITIES FACE TOUGH CHOICES: COMPARISON AND CONTRAST

We will begin with the New York Times piece from December of 2011. With the site of the concerns about CDBG being Allentown, Pennsylvania, the reporter (Michael Cooper) outlines key concerns about the importance of the program and, in doing so, provides plenty of information to be concerned about not only the fate of cities in this country but, more importantly, the fate of how the demise of these cities – including Omaha – will impact race relations.

Let us begin with the story and my analysis

> ALLENTOWN, Pa. — It is no secret that these are hard times for
> cities, with tax collections down, state aid dwindling, unemployment

> high and foreclosures pitting many blocks. So, as he sat in his office
> here, Mayor Ed Palowski of Allentown echoed the question mayors
> around the country are asking: Why has Washington cut one of the
> main federal programs for cities by a quarter in the last couple of
> years? (Cooper, 2011)

The logic expressed above is not consistently applied and it certainly isn't applied to the people who need it the most. For instance, the Mayor in the preceding excerpt is whining about "state aid dwindling" and other concerns. But all he has to do is move some money – money that is not his – around, fire some people and keep his job, which is probably paying him more than $100,000 a year. But what about poor people? What can we do when our household incomes start to "dwindle"? Who can we depend on? It certainly is not the local planning departments who receive free money based on our poverty. If they want to keep receiving it, the city has to have a "pocket of poverty;" and that pocket of poverty, no matter where you go for the most part, is US!

Continuing with the pity party:

> "It's just insane," an exasperated-sounding Mayor Pawlowski said.
> The shrinking federal program, called Community Development Block
> Grants, was devised by the Nixon administration to bypass state
> governments and send money directly to big cities, which were given
> broad leeway to decide how to spend it. This year the federal
> government is giving out just $2.9 billion — a billion dollars less than
> it gave two years ago, and even less than it gave during the Carter
> administration, when the money went much further. Here in Allentown
> the steadily shrinking funds mean that there will be hard choices ahead.
> (Cooper, 2011).

Sending money to big cities was the mistake: when the Mayors of those cities saw those checks, they lost their damn minds. These white men started rewriting the rules so that they can peel off of the allocations whatever amounts they wanted in order to build suburbs, change their skylines, hire their own people, create loan programs and the like. All the while they lost track of the ghetto, whose povery qualified them for the money in the first place. Tokenism, the funding of "negroes" who they could control, was the order of the day. Every city getting CDBG money has an individual or an organization that occupies this "niggerologist" position.

The key to the preceding paragraph is the concept of "broad leeway." Since that time, the funding process has reverted to the states who then send the money to cities. But in states like Wisconsin and Nebraska, where there is only one major black community (Milwaukee and Omaha, respectively) or one major poverty area (the Native Americans in these states take care of themselves through the Bureau of Indian Affairs and their casinos), it's simple for the states to send money to the major city and then blow the rest of it on their white pals, counterparts, developers and so on.

Finally, any "hard choices" that have to be made by any city getting this free money would be easy to make: just cut back the bullshit you spend on a previous allocation! All the pals you hired, all the palms you've greased, all the bullshit recreational facilities you constructed to appease minorities – cut that shit and start spending the money on job creating programs that hire minorities. So far in both of the cities mentioned above, these white people want to create an oasis of their downtown areas and not hire any minority contractors to do the work. When they do hire some, it's for a pittance and crumbs while the white developers get contracts for skyscrapers, miles of fencing and massive renovations of housing.

Take note of the following:

> The grants have helped pay for the tidy new facades on restaurants like Casa Latina and Winston's West Indian & American Restaurant on Seventh Street, which have been credited with sprucing up the neighborhood and drawing college students downtown to eat. They have paid for inspections of 1,500 homes in the city's poorest wards, and for repairs of some. And recently, behind a door with an orange "Unfit for Human Habitation" sticker on it, they paid a crew to do a gut rehab of a blighted row house at the edge of a blossoming historic district. (Cooper, 2011).

Token allocations to fix facades on minority restaurants. Just great. But what about the poverty-related problems that qualified the city for the grants in the first place? Again, if they address those problems, they won't qualify for CDBG the following year. Somebody has to stay poor: so it's going to be US! And you wonder why black communities around the nation continue to look the same or actually decline from year to year when the government is allocating millions. I'm showing you how it's done and why it's done.

Notice that the grant pays for inspections of homes and "for repairs of some." Why not all of them? How do they choose which ones they are going to repair? If the homes are rented, the white landlord gets the money and by fixing up his home, they increase the value of it. What about the low-income people who are living in it? What do they get? Then they boast about the gutting of ONE row house at the edge of a blossoming historic district. Again, that is self-serving: by fixing up that house they upgrade the historic district in general. Again, the people whose poverty is in question are overlooked once that giant check arrives in the city coffers. And it's going on all over the nation.

I came up with a concept that I call "The Toys For Tots Syndrome." Every year, usually around Thanksgiving and Christmas, these white people start giving away consumable stuff in the name of charity. From turkeys and Christmas trees to school supplies, they give away stuff that will be eaten, thrown away or, in some way, "consumed." Then, the people who got it are right back where they started. This seems to be the modus operandi of cities and their applications of various parts of the grant money as it relates to low income areas and minorities. For example,

> The money is not just for brick-and-mortar projects. It pays for two after-school teachers at St. Luke's Neighborhood Center, where a couple of dozen children, some homeless, spent a recent afternoon making artwork by gluing pompoms to strips of foam. And it helps pay for the Daybreak program, a drop-in center for people with mental illness or substance abuse problems, where a couple of dozen people spent the afternoon watching "Mr. Magoo's Christmas Carol" on a big-screen television while workers scurried around the kitchen, which serves three meals a day. But with its share of the grant halved in recent years, to $15,000, Daybreak is looking for savings. (Cooepr, 2011)

The fact is, the money was not solely for bricks-and-mortar in the first place. The Housing and Community Development act of 1974 was concerned about the environment of a low-income area: it provided for job development, actual employment, social services and so on. But when cities found out that they had discretion, they flipped the script and started funding only those things that would return money back to THEM. So for every house renovated, they could generate tax revenue; for every downtown structure they built, businesses were attracted and as a result, more taxes. It was all about taking the free money they got from the government and making more money for themselves. While all this went on, the poor remained poor and in most cases, got even poorer.

Cities that receive millions offer crumbs to the poor. Instead of paying for two after school teachers are a local center, why not hire ten or twelve full time, year round? Token programs seem to be the best that these cities have to offer the low-income areas and the unemployed people who the grant was designed to serve. And HUD knows about all this – but refuses to act because if it does, its own lack of monitoring, evaluation and oversight would come into question. And then the people who work for HUD or the Office of the Inspector General for HUD would come under fire. They are not about to risk their jobs just to defend poor people (many of whom don't vote). So the cities keep getting their way, keep neglecting low-income areas and keep exploiting the poverty situation. And then, every once in a while, a major TV network will carry a "special report" as to "is the war on poverty working?"

The CDBG plot begins to thicken:

> "We do stand the chance of having to cut a staff member," said the Rev. Dr. Christine L. Nelson, the executive director of the Lehigh County Conference of Churches, which runs Daybreak, who said other sources of money were drying up as well. "That would be very difficult because with this kind of program, we only have five as it is, and we need to keep two on the floor at all times for safety's sake, for the clients' safety." (Cooper, 2011)

These people are abusing CDBG funding. These nickel-and-dime operations that only meet the needs of the few should not be getting this free money. I could understand food pantries, homeless shelters or veterans centers, but some church-based organization, which gets money from the poor as it is (by way of Sunday collections) shouldn't be sucking from the teet of City government. What happened to the separation of church and state? Oh, that's right: the separation exists unless it comes down to money. And when money comes into the picture all of a sudden it's "in God we trust"!

More abuse is on the way as the following excerpt bears out:

> Cuts to the block grants program were cited in a recent report by the nonpartisan Government Accountability Office, which noted that the number of vacant properties in America has jumped to 10 million from 7 million in 2000, threatening to attract crime and cause blight. "With sustained high foreclosure and unemployment rates and further declining home values, local officials said that continued, flexible C.D.B.G. funding would help them maintain efforts to address vacant properties in their areas," the report noted. (Cooper, 2011).

Vacant properties are the result of neglect and racism. People lived in these houses at one time. Because unemployment is so high, many people had to move out or go to homeless shelters. When these houses are abandoned, derelicts, dope friends, drunks and other homeless individuals use them for crash pads. And that is how they remain vacant. Add to that city neglect, knowing full well that such houses also attract rats, roaches, tall weeds that present a danger to young girls and so on. Do they care? Of course not. The city planners don't live in the low-income communities that they are supposed to be servicing.

While they "talk" about blight in these areas, cities like Omaha make up a "blight designation" so that they can receive tax incremental financing and build mega-structures. The area where the Mid-City Park , the Element Hotel and a movie theatre are now located was an area that was labeled "blighted." There was no blight – just city planners playing games. Even now they are taking a major mall and plan to turn it into a development that includes high rent condos. How did they pave the way for this project? By claiming that the mall is in a "blighted" area.

The lie that these people tell is akin to what the Mayor claimed: that CDBG money could help them "maintain their efforts" to do whatever it is they were doing. But their efforts are not aimed at the area that is most in need and therefore those efforts SHOULD be terminated with extreme prejudice. If black people don't get paid, then THEY (white folks and the planning departments) shouldn't be getting paid off the fact that black folks aren't being paid. It's as simple as that.

Even the critics seem to be taking their time taking what they know and filing grievances and suits against the CDBG program, their local planning departments and HUD. Even after bringing these abuses to the attention of the city council, county board and state of Nebraska in 1995, *nothing was done.* After doing it again this year, the Office of the Inspector General has yet to respond, and the Appropriations Committee of the Nebraska legislature has done nothing. A state has backward and poor as Nebraska needs all the grant money it can get, and its largest black community represents the "pocket of poverty" that the State needs in order keep its social service departments housing departments and health departments functioning. The sicker black people get, the richer white folks in Nebraska get.

> The program has its share of critics. The flexibility that so endears it to mayors and county executives has sometimes led to terrible misuses of the money, and even to criminal fraud. Policing the program has become a cottage industry for federal investigators, who have found money squandered over the years on foolish projects and on things like company picnics, gifts and bonuses, and who have won quite a few indictments related to the grants. (Cooper, 2011).

But the fact is that those who were in charge of "policing" were falling down on the job themselves. Everybody is so obsessed with getting paid and it seems that the key to getting paid is to see to it that low-income people don't get paid. The worse off the ghetto or barrio, the more deplorable the statistics, the bigger the Federal check. And then it becomes a spree. But we cannot lose sight of one fundamental fact.

This method of operation, this "strategy" of benefitting off of the backs of the poor and minority is nothing new. Ever since we nearly burned the country down back in the 1960s (I'm talking more about the black power movement than I am the more palatable civil rights movement), white folks figured they would make money off of us through the back door. Welfare, in my view, was the closest thing to reparations that we will ever come. But the real money was being made by the people who administered the program, accompanied by poverty pimp agencies like the Community Action Agencies. Another block grant, the Community Service Block Grant, was the social service version of the Community Development Block Grant.

Back in the late 1970s-early 1980s there was also something called the Urban Development Block Grant. It paved the way for a few local programs but was merged with the CDBG which meant more money for local municipalities. One man's "misuse" of funding was another man's treasure trove. If money was indeed "squandered over the years on foolish projects," then that is the government's fault: this means that there were repeated actions that were in violation of the rules and the government continued to allow it to take place.

Even the formula gives the city governments who are neglecting black communities a way out:

> And the complicated formulas used to divide the money among about 1,200 local governments — based on population, poverty, the age of housing stock and overcrowding — have been criticized as not sending the money to the neediest communities. (Cooper, 2011).

And how do they make sure that they keep qualifying under the formula outlined above? The on-going abuse of their black and minority populations, that's how. In terms of population, they annex nearby suburban communities to add more people to their populations and as such, qualify for increasing amounts of grant dollars (annexation also means more property taxes, sales taxes and other revenue can be generated).

Poverty: simply keep manipulating the poor and denying them jobs so that the only income comes from the departments of social services. Poverty, as the old saying taught, creates a race of beggars. As for "age of the housing stock" – simply do nothing to renovate or improve it, and allow it to age. And as for "overcrowding," continue to manipulate the environment and in almost every city in America, the highest population density (people per square acre) can be found in black and minority communities. The formula has therefore been complied with and these cities can get that free money by manipulating the very low-income populations that they purport to serve.

Once you make sure that the poor remain poor, segregated and rooted in high population density (which also leads to increased conflict), then you can spend the money on whatever you want to:

But mayors see it as an invaluable tool — one of the few federal
programs that sends money directly to big cities, without going through
the middlemen at the state level. Before its creation, mayors had to
apply for small grants in many specific areas — leading to complaints
of the this-food-is-terrible-and-the-portions-are-so-small variety. Tom
Cochran, the executive director of the United States Conference of
Mayors, said that mayors were thrilled when the Nixon administration
agreed to consolidate the various grants into a single block grant
program, which could be used broadly for community development,
with local officials choosing their priorities. It was signed into law by
President Gerald R. Ford. (Cooper, 2011)

Two criminals paved the way for today's "free-for-all" when it comes to
cities abusing CDBG funds. First, Nixon and his criminal behavior regarding the
Watergate break-ins and then signed into law by President Ford (of Omaha, of
course), who let Nixon off the hook – another crime. Conceived and
institutionalized by minds like these, is there any wonder why the CDBG program
is just as scatter-brained and rife with fraud as its leading policymakers?

Next come the justifications and cover ups for the abuse of these hundreds of
millions of dollars:

"It's been the mainstay of support for urban America across the board,"
Mr. Cochran said. The money each city gets may seem small —
Allentown got $2.5 million this year, a small sliver of its $89 million
budget — but mayors say that the money, and the freedom to decide
how to spend it, makes a big difference. (Cooper, 2011)

The CDBG program has been a "mainstay of support for urban America
across the board," the head man for the Council of Mayors claims. Yes, generally it
has. The inner city and low income areas of those "urban areas" have remained
poor while these mayors have used that money to do their own thing. They've
become so small that when cuts to the grants are threatened, they wine, or have
major newspapers write about all the "good" that has been done – the way the
Omaha World Herald did (this newspaper owns almost every single newspaper in
the state). They talk about those who received welfare as "leeches," but look at
their own actions on a much larger level and these men give a whole new meaning
to the word "parasite."

As a result of messing with their little play money, it should be no surprise
that these mayors would be pissed:

So mayors were furious when Congress cut the grants program last
month to $2.9 billion, a cut of 25 percent over two years. President
Obama had sought to reduce the program, too, but by less: his budget

proposal had called for a 7.5 percent cut. "This is a tough choice that balances the need to decrease the budget deficit with the tough fiscal conditions confronting state and local governments," the proposal said. (Cooper, 2011)

If the states and subsequently the cities, are not doing right by the people whose poverty qualified them for the grant money in the first place, and if such actions have been taking place for decades, then on these facts alone the program should be cut and so should HUD's allocations. HUD has been screwing up for some time in a number of areas and the poor would be better off marching and protesting in the streets (or worse) than waiting for the government to do right by them. When it comes to CDBG, the city planners and mayors are laughing at low income communities all the way to the bank.

This was in Allentown, Pennsylvania, which is much smaller than Omaha. But abuse of CDBG funds are taking place in Milwaukee, a city that was so lax in its allocation of funds that a decade ago a woman started a fly-by-night neighborhood association, made her daughter director if it, and clipped the city's CDBG funds for $60,000. This was just the tip of the iceberg. Another group known as North Milwaukee Neighborhood Residents was getting hundreds of thousands and giving it to a husband and wife team to renovate housing and, every year, they fell short. When the city dogged them or confronted them, they shouted "racism" and got the community into an uproar. In far too many cases the Planners caved.

When it's time for the guts, the planners and mayors want to once again use black people as scapegoats in a kind of "we can't help the negroes if you cut our budget" – as if they were helping poor people in the first place. According to the article that is being cited from, it concludes, thusly: "It has really helped us limit blight, and rebuilt some of our poorest neighborhoods," Mayor Pawlowski said. "With the continual reduction of this funding, we're able to do less and less." (Cooper, 2011).

Let us move on.

The next article appeared a few months later (May 2012) in *the San Gabriel Valley Tribune*. Written by J.D. Velasaco, the article offered the following (along with my commentary and critique).

People for People thrift shop volunteer Alma Cristol, left, bags clothing for a homeless client March 28, 2012. The San Gabriel homeless assistance program is expecting a loss of funding due to reduced federal assistance at the Mission Road facility. (SGVN/Staff photo by Leo Jarzomb). With federal funding for community programs and services being slashed by Congress, cities across the

> region are facing tough decisions about which local programs to
> keep and which ones to let go. (Velasco, 2012)

Again, we find the "Toys for Tots" syndrome in effect. Don't get me wrong: I support homeless shelters and the like because they deal directly with the poor. But it's all about consumption: they help people who then leave and then many of them replicate the social security numbers associated with the beds that the homeless use. This is done to keep the money going; many of them do it so I know what I'm talking about. People need help, but when the CDBG was first created, in association with the Housing and Community Development Act of 1974, it was about providing jobs and social support so that people could afford to get into their own houses. It was about affordable housing and social services. The local programs financed by CDBG are usually run by pals and cronies of the local planning department. HUD knows it – but hardly ever acts until the abuse of the funding reaches crisis proportions.

More information follows:

> San Gabriel Valley cities are scrambling to deal with cuts of 25 to
> 35 percent to their Community Development Block Grant funds -
> which help pay for everything from parks to graffiti abatement to
> food banks to housing programs for the needy. "I don't think people
> realize how much the program has been cut," said Bill Huang,
> Pasadena housing director. (Velasco, 2012)

My house concerned about CDBG the people in administrative and managerial positions become when THEIR paychecks are threatened! These poverty pimps (which is what they are for the most part) get off by making people think that they care about "the needy and the poor." But if those paychecks get cut out, let's see how much these same people are willing to volunteer their time to "help." I guarantee you it won't happen; they pray that poverty and bad luck continues so that they can continue to deal with inner city issues. Where there is graffiti there are gangs. Where there are food banks there are poor people. Graffiti abatement means a job for some white person – how could it be full time? But that's what CDBG is allowing these localities to get away with. And after all that energy and effort is expended, do the ranks of the poor diminish? No.Poverty is built into the American capitalist system – haves and have nots, remember?

Let us reflect back to and recall what the purpose of the CDBG funding was, and you'll see how today, it is in the hands of white people who are making decisions for black people. Take note:

> Since 1974, the federal government has provides cities, counties and
> states with CDBG funding. Local governments are mostly free to

use the funding as they see fit, provided it benefits the community in some way. "The purpose of CDBG is to give state and local governments a resource to do their own community development work," said Brian Sullivan, a spokesman for the Department of Housing and Urban Development, which administers CDBG funding. (Velasco, 2012)

The key to the statement above is where it states that "Local governments are mostly free to use the funding as they see fit." That's the only part that these cities seem to understand; they don't seem to get the fact that the statement continues by outlining that they can do as they please **"provided it benefits the community in some way."** Who is best qualified to decide what the community wants or needs? Of course it would be the community or a representative of that community.

So what these cities do in many cases, in addition to their token "negro" or "minority" leaders, is set up these shill operations to function in the name of low-income people. Sometimes the token negro or minority "leaders" that were committed to the city would help in the set up. In Omaha there was a group called North Omaha Community Development that fulfilled this function. In exchange for obedience they were paid out of the city's coffers and even had their offices renovated. In Milwaukee, so-called "militant activist" leader Michael McGee got CDBG funding for Project Respect, a group that did little or nothing but hang out in a red, black and green building on the eastern border of the black community. Almost every major city has such a shill that does its bidding in the name of the black, minority or low income area.

Inevitably, the free money from the government would dry up (as do all good things it seems):

> But with Congress increasingly interested in cutting federal spending and reducing the deficit, during the past two years it has cut a total of $1 billion from the program. That amounts about a quarter of the funding the program was receiving. And with the pie shrinking, each city that takes part in the program is getting a smaller slice. (Velasco, 2012)

A smaller slice of money they don't deserve. After showing, for years, that they weren't going to do right by the poor and minority, the money should have been shut off right then and there. But HUD, in all of its ineptitude, just kept on doling it out as Congressmen and Senators fought to keep the money coming so that they could "brag" about it and then win re-election. In simpler terms, everybody seems to be getting paid except for the people whose poverty led to the creation and maintenance of the program in the first place.

Sounding like pirates splitting up their ill-gotten booty, check out the following paragraph:

> El Monte's CDBG funding will drop by 20 percent next year, from $3.5 million to $2.8 million. The City Council was expected to discuss how that money would be divvied up at its meeting Tuesday night. City Manager Rene Bobadilla said city staff was going to recommend that existing community programs be kept intact, albeit at reduced funding levels. "We're going to have to really look at how far the dollars are going," Bobadilla said. (Velasco, 2012)

Check out the terminology: "The City Council was expected to discuss how that money would be divvied up at its meeting Tuesday night." Where was the community input? Where were the community development specialists? Why was the City Council making all the decisions? On what basis were their decisions made? This is the kind of elitist and oligarchal decision making that I have charged with most of these cities: between the planning department and the city council, the masses of people never get a fair shot at inclusion. And as we know, "to divide the process is to deform the product."

Continuing:

> In Whittier, where CDBG funds are used to pay for social services for the poor and senior citizens, as well repairs for dilapidated homes, the funding level is going to drop by 25 percent. "All of those are going to take a hit," said Community Development Director Aldo Schindler. (Velasco, 2012)

At least Whittier is dealing with social services aspects of CDBG. Places like Milwaukee and Omaha provide funding to organizations who, in turn, are expected to spend it wisely. But how can you be expected to do a good job when poverty is the key to your paycheck? As long as there is no community advisory board intact, the decisions are going to be made based on a race-based buddy system. And in such a context, black people can only lose.

The key word is "demographics," as the following excerpt explains:

> But not all of the cuts in CDBG funding can be blamed on Congress, Sullivan of HUD said. Some cities are receiving less money because the demographics have changed. Rosemead, for example, is seeing its CDBG funding drop from $1 million last year to $682,000 this year.

By "demographics" they're not just talking about race or ethnicity. They're talking about compartmentalization or dispersal. If the community's poor are moving out to other areas of the city, that breaks up the "pocket of poverty" that is one of the elements of the CDBG formula. Demographics change which is why so many cities are working to annex surrounding areas so that their populations can increase. As long as the increase means poor people, there is a chance that they will keep their checks; but as socioeconomic status grows, the chances for on-going CDBG checks decrease. What we are talking about is "demographic transition:" from low-income to middle class, from black to white and from high density to "average" density.

Want proof? Take the case of Rosemead, California:

> Sullivan said the cut is in part because HUD recalculated how much money Rosemead should get based on new census data.
> And according to data from the American Community Survey, the number of people living in poverty in Rosemead dropped by more than 5,000 from 2010 to 2011. During that same period, the number of overcrowded housing units in the city decreased by nearly 3,000. Both of those numbers are used to determine how much CDBG money a city should receive. (Velasco, 2012)

And so it goes. If they tell the truth about their community they stand to lose a free check from the Feds. So don't think for one minute that these white people won't lie or figure out a way to fudge the data. They can pretend that they didn't know about the movement or that they were busy "processing" the census data. Recently in Omaha it came to light that for several years the police department "forgot" to submit data that had to do with black homicides. Forgot! This convenient omission of facts, this "selective amnesia" has been used for decades to cover up abuse of funds. But because most communities are too uninvolved, apathetic or ignorant of what is taking place behind the closed doors of their "representatives," the abuse of Federal funding continues. The fact that HUD is turning their heads to these facts doesn't help out the masses of people, either.

What is the "we-didn't-do-it" response?

> "Obviously we are always changing as a nation, and as the nation changes, so does the data," Sullivan said. That's little consolation to some of the groups that rely on the CDBG funds to pay for their operations. (Velasco, 2012)

Sullivan seems to be passing the buck when he says that, "as the nation changes, so do the data." A more accurate statement would be, "as the white decision makers change, so they act accordingly to manipulate the nation and the data." There is no national input into what the planners and mayors do because there is no local input. They simply cheat for as long as they can, and when the demographics change, they come up with new ways to change the rules while at the same time pretending that they did nothing wrong.

In conclusion,

> The Rosemead City Council on Tuesday also discussed what to do with its limited CDBG resources. "Unfortunately, the drastic cuts to these federal programs will prohibit the funding of many previously funded activities while others will be severely reduced," according to a staff report. (Velasco, 2012)

These leeches at the city level – mayors and planners – have been so dependent on CDBG funds that they act as if it is the fault of the government when the cuts come. It is part of the role of a good administrator to be able to read trends and determine if cuts are on the way, to anticipate such cuts in a turbulent economy such as this. Instead, kicking back by the pool and playing with the remote controls to their garage door openers, they act as if things will always be good. And if they get bad, simply pass the major pain and cuts down to the poor while making sure that YOUR paycheck, mortgage, cow payment and kids' tuition remains intact.

THE GRANT, THE GREED, THE GROTESQUE "GIVEAWAYS"

An article titled, "Block Grants Forever: A Deathless Program and its Long History of Failure" is the perfect backdrop for what is taking place in Omaha, how North Omaha became and continues to be "under developed" and why those in power worry about and continue to leech for continuation of the grant program. This articles provides much needed history that I will then juxtapose with what is taking place in Omaha during the same periods to show that the abuse of CDBG was a collective abuse, and that Omaha has been and continues to be just as guilty and culpable as much larger cities and the ones mentioned in the aforementioned article.

We find that,

> [In 2010] … a federal judge decided to let the Association of Community Organizations for Reform Now (Acorn) continue receiving money through the federally funded Community Development Block Grant program (CDBG). Critics of the controversial activist group were outraged: after all, Congress had banned it from participating in federal programs after embarrassing videos showed its mortgage counselors advising undercover journalists on how to break the law. As it turns out, the judge's decision probably won't be enough to

> keep Acorn from going out of business. But the real outrage
> is that CDBG still exists. (Malanga, 2010)

ACORN was putting in work and I met some members briefly when I lived in Chicago back in 1987. At any rate, this goes to show you: when activist groups get ahold of a good grant writer and can garner some community support, they can get funding and do some great things. This is what I tried to do with a major neighborhood association, the largest black group in the state of Nebraska putting in work at the neighborhood level, and named after the poorest zip code in the black community. That zip code is 68111, hence the name "Triple One Neighborhood Association and Parents' Union." We also addressed educational issues, hence the "parents union" component.

And grass roots groups do this better than those administrative laissez-faire agencies that local governments tend to fund. Grass roots groups are "right there" on the front lines with the people who need the services; these other groups are nothing more than poverty pimps; they do just enough to justify their existence, but since most of their programs are not outcome based, there is no way to really know if they've moved a group or an individual from point "a" to point "b." They just claim that they have and the government is so lazy that they don't bother to check; after all, it's only the "niggers" (that seems to be their logic).

According to the previous excerpt there were videos of what ACORN was doing. Why don't the people at HUD or the ones administering the CDBG money spend some time taping themselves in the act of scamming. Why don't they tape those decision-making meetings where they decide to ignore the impoverished areas of the city and instead, spend money on swimming pools, parks, and projects in the suburban part of town?

Continuing:

> Nearly four decades old, CDBG has dished out some $120
> billion in local grants over the years, with little to show for
> all that taxpayer money. Designed initially as a community-
> rebuilding and antipoverty effort, CDBG doesn't require its
> beneficiaries to prove that they are, in fact, improving their
> local communities or reducing poverty. As a result, the
> program has evolved into little more than a congressional
> patronage tool, a free ride for politically connected social
> programs that have never demonstrated their effectiveness,
> and a way for municipal politicians to finance their favorite
> schemes when their own budgets come under pressure.
> (Malanga, 2010).

It's easy money. While these white folks were whining and crying about black people getting welfare ("welfare cheats,""welfare Cadillacs," "welfare chiselers," "leeches") and so on, these white folks, at the city level, were getting paid some REAL money!

If the goal were truly "community building" and "antipoverty," then where were the outcomes and controls? Where was the annual monitoring or supervision? As welfare and other social programs continue to show, only programs that are geared toward the low-income and minority are ignored or left to fend for themselves, or left at the mercy of the 'discretion" of those who are supposed to be in charge. And why is that the case? So that they can fail and once exposed, the minorities and low-income can be blamed for the lack of success. The fact that these programs keep getting funded, even during the most financially strapped of times, proves that it's a scam manipulated by city administrations. But nobody does a thing.

Can a system condemn itself? Of course not. And that is the key to the CDBG boondoggle and,by extension, the failure of programs like CDBG to operate in cities like Omaha, Nebraska. The fear of what black people would do to this country (just like the black people in Ferguson, Missouri scared the shit out of the entire state) was felt by the administration and something had to be done. In simpler terms,

> The CDBG program was a reaction to the Johnson administration's Great Society efforts, which had tried to use massive federal spending to rebuild deteriorating urban neighborhoods, stimulate local economies, and even stitch together the sense of community that was disappearing from inner cities. Johnson's successor, Richard Nixon, decided to contain the vast federal bureaucracy that these programs had spawned by giving money directly to states and cities, where local politicians would administer it. Congress and the Nixon administration accordingly gave localities wide discretion in how to spend the money. (Malanga, 2010)

The writers of social history are particular about what they say; they never want to give credit to people of color and the major role we played in molding this country. Johnson's so-called "Great Society," just like the efforts by Kennedy before him, were all a result of black people threatening to burn this country down. One the one hand you had Martin Luther King, Jr. and the civil rights movement: marching, protesting, praying in public and taking ass whippings in front of the world and embarrassing the hell out of America in the process. On the other hand, you had the black power movement: chanting, burning, confronting cops, sniping and threatening white folks on a physical level. Between the two the white administration had to respond. It is at this point that the Great Society and all those efforts that followed – civil rights acts, model cities programs, urban renewal, affirmative action, equal opportunity and so on – came into play. So don't get it twisted: white fear brought about changes, and black initiative was the basis of that fear.

If an on-going collection of black men were charged with a program that failed time after time, even a moron would come to the conclusion that black people should not be running such programs. But when it comes to white boys, one presidential administration after another tries and fails but in each failure, they continue to put other white boys in charge. And the reason why they fail is simple: they don't know what in the FUCK they're doing. All they know is that when it comes to black people, the end result or the outcome has to be a negative one. In that way, they can continue to keep the poverty money coming.

When you give any person "wide discretion," the result is going to be self-serving. That's how people are. If you gave Asians wide discretion to administer poverty money, they would help Asians first. If you gave women wide discretion over a massive budget, women would benefit first. If a white man has wide discretion, he goes beyond merely seeing to it that his people benefit; there also has to be an initiative or endeavor that also guarantees black subjugation.

And that is just what happened with the Community Development Block Grant program:

> The Nixonites' faith in local officials now seems quaint,
> considering the way they began manipulating the program
> almost immediately. Often ignoring the most distressed
> communities, local pols channeled the grants into their pet
> projects, including tennis courts and parks in affluent areas,
> purchases of CB radios and other perks for senior-citizen
> centers, and new roads and other infrastructure improvements
> in thriving neighborhoods. (Malanga, 2010)

If these local officials began manipulating the program "almost immediately," then where was the oversight? It's been almost forty years and these localities keep on repeating the same thing: using CDBG funds to improve communities that are already strong, virtually ignoring minority and low-income communities (offering only token crumbs to the ones that do their bidding and cover up for them) and hire their friends and relatives. This has been doing on ever since the inception of the program! Because of this fact, we can no longer write off what has happened as "bad management," "poor allocations" or "inadequate program planning." The actions of these people have been and continue to be **totally by design.**

Additional evidence is provided below:

> Officials claimed that this spending would provide
> employment to the poor, though there was never any
> evidence of that. The widespread abuse of the program
> prompted immediate calls for reform. In 1976, presidential
> candidate Jimmy Carter complained about "frivolous" uses of
> the federal aid and promised changes. But once elected,
> Carter realized that CDBG could be a formidable political
> tool; rather than reform it, he vastly expanded the grants so
> that any community in America could qualify for them …
> (Malanga, 2010)

They were all in it, those at the top on a national, regional and local basis. It seemed that the key to maintaining white employment was to enhance and maintain black unemployment. The more pain felt in the ghetto and barrio, the more programs could be created to create more jobs for whites. Today, it's the prison system: the more blacks arrested the more prisons needed, the more white security guards, wardens, cooks, janitors, and office walkers needed at those prisons. That's why they build these prisons in small towns: that's where the most simple and most racist Americans are to be found.

Keep blacks poor and keep the city coffers full was the formula, or so it seemed. Furthermore,

> In doing so, he won the support of Washington Republicans
> as well as Democrats and of small-town councils as well as
> big-city mayors. This widespread backing helped insulate the
> program from efforts by Carter's successor, Ronald Reagan,
> to kill it. (Malanga, 2010)

White men fighting over black issues – just like they did when they were dividing up Africa. Just like they did when they would stage "slave battles" and find out whose servant was the toughest and therefore, whose plantation was number one. Just like they do today in the same way with football and basketball at both the collegiate and professional levels. Make black people think that they care about them when the decisions of these white men clearly show the opposite.

And as was and remains the case in sports and any big money competition, you will find illegality and scandal. As Malanga (2010) put it,

> Block grants soon became a national scandal. In the 1980s,
> an investigation by the general counsel of the Department of
> Housing and Urban Development found rampant favoritism
> in awarding the grants and disclosed that members of

> Congress were using the program for their own pet projects
> inserted into HUD's appropriations bills, from sugarcane
> mills in Hawaii to a library and recreation center on
> Mackinac Island in Michigan to a county courthouse in
> Newport, Washington.

So HUD found wrongdoing as far back as the 1980s. But what was done. Were there sanctions? Fines? Did anyone do time? Of course not. And the American people didn't do a damn thing about it, just as now and today Omahans, black and white, stand idly by and watch all my research and work to expose and sue the City of Omaha go to waste. All I can hope to do is preserve a record that someone else, perhaps decades down the road, will find and then re-ignite because assuredly, the violations by the City Planning Department of CDBG money are going to exist as long as the program itself does.

Moving right along:

> A few years later, President Clinton's transition team
> criticized the program for "systematic plunder of many
> millions of taxpayer dollars." Still, when big-city mayors
> who had backed Clinton presented him with a list of projects
> that were "ready to go" if he could find the funding, the new
> president proposed a $2.5 billion increase in block grants.
> And though Clinton promised to clean up the program, a
> 1999 audit by the General Accounting Office found that
> CDBG was in worse shape than ever. (Malanga, 2010).

Clinton lied but he was no worse than his predecessors – they were all "allowing" HUD to give out money and then turn their heads as the cities spent it on whatever they wanted. And when they did it, poverty was stabilized, ensured and in most cases, got worse. Did they care? Of course not. Were they being watched? Of course not. Just as Clinton saw the wrongs that were being committed but because of "politics" went ahead and funded the program with an increase, President Bush did something similar. Check it out:

> Realizing CDBG's sorry track record, the George W. Bush
> administration tried to cut its funding significantly and
> redirect what would be left of the program into narrower,
> more focused, economic-development projects in poorer
> neighborhoods. Bush's Office of Management and Budget
> even proposed new standards to evaluate the effectiveness of
> such programs, including requiring measurable results like
> declining poverty rates and rising income levels. (Malanga,
> 2010).

This sounds like a strategy: an outcome based measurement that would deal with success rather than the typical "blank check" approach. But that's all talk – check out what ended up taking place:

> But Congress resisted making changes, and Bush's critics,
> ignoring the long history of CDBG ineffectiveness, blasted
> the president for wanting to slash aid to cities. Former
> Baltimore mayor Martin O'Malley ludicrously compared the
> proposed cuts to a terrorist attack. The program has survived
> one damning report and investigation after another.
> (Malanga, 2010)

Congress – made up of people who were voted in by the people who live in their states, usually the largest cities of those states. Those largest cities are the recipients of CDBG grants, and they want to keep that money flowing. So what did Bush expect: for cities to collectively decide that they wanted to finally "do the right thing" by the poor and minority? Please!

The program has survived in the same way that racism and discrimination have survived. Even though it may cost the government in terms of lawsuits and so on, all of these keep going because they tend to appease and satisfy so many white people. The key is to "keep the blacks under control and in THEIR community," and racism, discrimination and the allocations of CDBG grants by local municipalities tend to do just that. That is how the CDBG program, no matter who is in office locally or directing HUD.

Moving right along:

> In 2004, a *Buffalo News* investigative series concluded that
> the city had squandered virtually all of the $550 million it
> had received in block-grant money since the 1970s—a
> significant discovery, considering that Buffalo had won more
> CDBG funding per capita than any other American
> community. The paper found that "city hall frittered away
> much of the money through parochial politics and
> bureaucratic ineptitude," an assessment that Buffalo officials
> didn't even dispute. (Malanga, 2010).

Over half a BILLION dollars blown by a hick-ass, mid-sized city. And despite what you just read, was there any penalty or any sanctions? Were there any fines? Did it make the national news? No. These white people do their dirt with taxpayer money and the white majority remains mum because it doesn't directly or negative affect THEM. After all, the money is supposed to "help the minorities" and therefore, the intentions were there. But they can't prove that there was any kind of morality behind the motives and as is said, "the road to hell is paved with good intentions.

Today, in 2014, there is a major deficit and a plethora of economic problems plaguing this country. And while there are cuts being made in social service programs all over the nation, the CDBG program, over the past thirty-plus years, has enriched white people, provided them with jobs, enhanced their recreational opportunities, fed their children, paid their mortgages and car notes and given them prestige in planning departments all over the nation. At the same time they've allowed low-income communities to continue to remain poor so that they (the city planning departments) could submit proposals to the Federal government that enable the money to keep coming in despite their piss-pot pour track records.

Put another way,

> The city's mayor, Anthony Masiello, told the *News* that CDBG was "a politically motivated system," while city council member Joseph Golombek, Jr. later said that local politicians were "pigs feeding at the trough" of the program. Left unanswered was why there had been so little federal oversight during all those years of abuse. (Malanga, 2010).

When white folks get caught ripping off their own, nothing happens. The more they steal it seems, the more likely they are to be punished while not getting "caught in the act." They may have to do a little time in a posh prison cell, but that is rare. When it comes to CDBG, I haven't heard of a single planning director or mayor being punished for abusing it. America, as a nation, is so egotistical, so arrogant and so corrupt, that the clock just keeps on ticking and the money, no matter how bad off the economy is, just keeps pouring in.

As I've said, other than his race, Obama is really no different. He's killing men of color all over the world just as his predecessors did, and he mouths those patriotic statements on a regular basis. Only black people, as a race, would allow him to get away with such bullshit (just like they did Marion Barry, Jesse Jackson, Gus Savage and so many other "negro leaders"):

> The CDBG program should be even safer under President Obama. As a presidential candidate in 2008, he described it as his Number One spending initiative for cities. The grants were "an important program that provides housing and creating [*sic*] jobs for low- and moderate-income people and places," Obama said. (Malanga, 2010).

Obama must have been reading the promotional material for the program, instead of basing his comments on what he's studied or what the outcomes of the

CDBG programs have been. Under Obama's watch, the pain felt by inner cities has continued on because he's not the one calling the shots – his job is just to carry out what his white "advisors" tell him to do. And while doing that, to also make sure that he satisfies all those people who went out and got people to vote for him. Those mayors who supported him are being rewarded with CDBG carte blanche. And it doesn't seem that anybody is doing anything about it.

The article concludes as follows:

> In the long history of CDBG, perhaps the most comical abuse of funds occurred when the mayor of a small Texas town illegally used tens of thousands of dollars to pay for psychic readings. While it's not recorded what the psychic told the mayor, it could very well have been something like this: "Your tenure, Mr. Mayor, is likely to be short. But block grants—they'll go on forever." (Malanga, 2010),.

Can there be such a thing as "comical abuse" when so many black and Latino people, so many low income people, are being ripped off? When so much housing is being torn down or neglected? When so many vacant lots in these inner cities remain filled with weeds and vermin? When so many streets are filled with potholes and street lights and sewers are in need of repair?

A MAYOR'S PLEA TO KEEP THE MONEY COMING

In February 2011, mayors all over issued various kinds of pleas to keep CDBG (read: free money) coming to their cities. Among those issuing what I call "leech letters," was the Mayor of Lewiston, Maine, Laurent F. Gilbert. His letter, which appeared in the February 19, 2011 issue of a Twin City newspaper in Maine, was titled, "Mayor's Corner: CDBG Funds Are of Tremendous Importance to Lewiston. Following is the full text of that article with my analyses filtering in and out as Gilbert's comments relate to what is taking place in Omaha, Nebraska, which seems to be the worst of the worst.

> A letter dated February 10, 2011 to members of Congress, sent from a coalition of the United States Conference of Mayors and nine other national organizations representing various forms of community development, offered the following facts: Based on data that grantees have reported to the Department of Housing and Urban Development over the past six years, the CDBG Program has …(Gilbert, 2011)

They offer "facts" in order to save their collective asses. But if they've lied thus far on the applications to the government, and if they've lied about what they intend to and have done with the grant money, then how can their easily assembled "facts" have any reliability or credibility? What do you expect them to produce – the truth? White folks have a way of "playing dumb" when they're listening to testimony or reading "facts" from their subordinates. They see what they want to see and hear what they want to hear. And that is how a corrupt system can be maintained and perpetuated over the decades.

And why are the data they claim to be providing only from the past SIX years? What about the other 24 years where CDBG was provided to most of these 1,209 cities? A partial record is tantamount to no real record at all in my book.

So let's look at, and then analyze, some of these facts as they relate to the claims provided by the Mayors and as they specifically impact on and reflect the reality in Omaha, Nebraska. According to the article,

> Assisted 865,874 low- and moderate-income households
> through single-family and multifamily residential
> rehabilitation, homeownership assistance, energy-efficient
> improvements and lead-based paint abatement;

Lumping all this together when each form of alleged "assistance" serves different functions. To rehabilitate a house can be the same thing as making it energy-efficient and removing lead-based paint. So they're comingling programs and in doing so, hope to increase their numbers. And what do they mean by "homeownership" assistance? Omaha has a program called Family Housing Assistance Services, constructed a 2-story building on the southwest corner of the black community's most historic community, and then leases out meeting room space to community groups and hasn't done much in the area of housing "assistance." How can they unless they are "assisting" suburbanites in coming back to the more affordable inner city?

For instance, in the name of "homeownership assistance," Omaha constructs a building with the free grant money, has ownership of the building, benefits from the rentals from the building (there are other businesses in the structure), offers free space to black lackey groups that do their bidding and all this in the name of helping the poor. And at no time does HUD check in on these "projects" to make sure that cities like Omaha are doing their job.

There is also the claim that these cities have,

> Created or retained 259,346 jobs for low- and moderate-
> income persons through a variety of economic development
> activities;

Again, intentionally being vague. To "create" a job is different from "retaining" one. How do you retain a job for someone? If they already have a job, then what did you do to make sure they kept it? And as for job creation. These cities are full of shit: they create jobs for people who DON'T live in the low-income communities that they are supposed to give priority to. They are providing jobs for their own people.

A case in point: there are sixteen (16) people working in the City of Omaha Planning Department who are paid from CDBG money. Only three of them are black. And yet all of that CDBG – over $4 million a year on average – is received based on black poverty and other negative demographics. So they may be creating jobs for people, and not the low and moderate income people they claim to be serving because if they did, the unemployment rate for black people in Omaha wouldn't be hovering near 25%!

There is the further claim that through CDBG these 1,209 city recipients across the nation,

> Benefitted 22,998,047 low- and moderate-income households through such public improvements as development of senior centers, centers for the disabled and handicapped, health and child care centers and parks and recreation facilities;

How do they know how many low- and moderate-income households "benefited"? What is the definition of a household and different households represent different numbers. How do they know a particular household benefited from a "public" improvement? Did all households participate or apply to a program? Of course not. They want to lump all groups – disabled, seniors, children – into one group and come up with an arbitrary number. This is such bullshit. If HUD had its shit together, it would demand specific numbers to include names and social security numbers. Anything short of that is nothing more than farcical.

According to the numbers provided, the CDBG program also

> Benefitted 73,863,286 low- and moderate-income households through such public services as employment training, youth services, crime awareness/prevention, fair housing activities, mental health services, and services for abused and neglected children ...

Wouldn't these "public services" also be a part of what was mentioned earlier in terms of senior centers, handicapped assistance and children's services? Are they "double-dipping"? As for "fair housing activities," how could that be the case when all of the top ten cities in America remain racially segregated. In fact, even Milwaukee (ranked number 17) and Omaha (ranked number 47) are racially segregated, with black people living in ghettos and Latinos living in nearby barrios? What is "fair" about that?

Programs for the abused and neglected children, mental health, crime prevention and the like – they are either falling short or totally failing. And how could they not? All of these areas are on the rise because the "programs" and "projects" that are created to deal with these programs cannot condemn themselves; they have to make sure that the numbers are there for them to "serve" so that they can continue working! It's about job creation, but not for the people whose poverty are generating these service programs: the jobs are being created for the service providers themselves!

The following may well be an outright lie:

> Every dollar of CDBG funding leverages $1.62 in non CDBG funding. Certainly the City of Lewiston has had and continues to need CDBG funding to meet some of the very needs articulated above. As an entitlement community with two of the poorest census tracks in the State of Maine, the dollars are put to good use. On average the amount coming from CDBG grants is generally around $ 1 million annually.

How does a dollar of free money only leverage a dollar sixty-two in "non-CDBG funding? How did they arrive at that figure? What is the source of the "non-CDBG funding? These people make up shit and expect the people who are reading or evaluating it to simply be too bored, lazy or apathetic to call into question the source of their bullshit statistics. The fact is, the money that these cities receive from the government is free and its given to them to help out areas and people that those who receive the money don't give a shit about. With free money, white discretion and racism all working hand-in-hand, that dollar from the government generates for more than a buck sixty two when you consider all the "fringe benefits" that come with that free dollar based on what that dollar is invested in (parks and recreation, streets, expanded suburbs, annexation proposals, jobs for white folks, new homes and cars for white folks, the taxes paid on what those white folks buy, and so on.

In the case of Lewiston, Maine, they receive about a million annually, according to the Mayor. But that's more than they deserve based on what they're doing for the people who need help the most. The City of Omaha has gotten about $217 million over the past 39 years and yet the area that it was supposed to help or improve is worse now than it was in 1975, unemployment in that area is higher now than it was in 1975, crime is higher now than it was in 1975 and so on. I am willing to bet that the same is true in the case of Lewiston.

So the mayor claims that they only get about a million a year? Let's see what they do with it:

> A few of the public services that have received CDBG
> assistance are: Abused Women's Advocacy Project;
> Advocates for Children-Healthy Families; American Red
> Cross-Disaster Services, Androscoggin Head Start & Child
> Care; Androscoggin Home Health-Lewiston Home Care;
> Lewiston Recreation Department Multi-Purpose Center After
> School Program; Museum L-A; Seniors Plus; St. Mary's
> Nutrition Center; Sexual Assault Crisis Center; Tri-County
> Mental Health Services; Trinity Jubilee Center; YWCA
> Intervention; Lewiston Police Department Enhanced
> Neighborhood Policing; and the list goes on.

All of these nonprofits do good work. But the fact is, they have budgets without any help from CDBG. They apply for CDBG money to supplement or add to their regular monies. And none of these programs is creating any jobs, nor are any of them targeted for people of color.

And check out that "Lewiston Police Department Enhanced Neighborhood Policing." That is a program that is probably also getting Weed and Seed Money along with those specialty grants that police departments apply for to cover police overtime. What is meant by "Enhanced Neighborhood Policing"? The money is supposed to be spent on providing for the bread-and-butter needs of low income and minority people and improving the communities. Recreation programs like the YWCA are just that – leisure programs. Mental health should be covered with and by different grant sources and the senior programs should be covered by social service grants such as the Community Service Block Grant.

Other items that were funded, according to the Mayor of Lewiston, are as follows:

> In the area of economic development, the Downtown
> Improvement Program and the Lewiston-Auburn Transit
> Busses (sic) have received funding. Neighborhood
> improvements have included downtown infrastructure
> improvements; downtown neighborhood improvements, St.
> Mary's Nutrition Center's Lots to Gardens/Gardens.

I was under the impression that the Department of Transportation was responsible for funding local transit systems – not CDBG money. Maybe that is a choice that they made in Lewiston, but I don't think it's universal. And as for that so-called "Downtown Improvement Program," this is the kind of thing that cities normally use to rip off the grant: they form a committee and then transform it into a program that is usually made up of people from the city, such as individuals from the Department of Tourism, Department of Commerce, Department of Public Relations and others. Then they promote downtown development and build a bunch of shit and then hire white developers and contractors. Black people get no jobs out of this – it's just an ego trip for that particular city.

Omaha had a slick mayor named Mike Fahey who tried to combine downtown with the south edge of the black community, the latter known as North Omaha. So he took the first two letters of downtown and then added a suffix of "NO" and the area that they targeted for development dollars became, "NoDo." NoDo consisted of night clubs, apartment lofts that black people could not afford, office space that included sky-high rents, and a giant baseball stadium. What in the FUCK does this have to do with helping out the low income?

Along similar lines Lewiston appears to have used a similar method of operation:

> Parks and Recreation programs have received City Park Improvement funding. CDBG funds have also addressed commercial rehabilitations to various properties throughout the city, as well as façade grants on Lisbon Street. Housing rehabilitation loans have been provided all over the city, as have downtown improvement loans.

Commercial rehabilitations? Façade grants? These are important, but again, the masses of people did not decide on this: these decisions were made by the city administration in lieu of taking their asses into the ghetto and making major chances in terms of the unemployment rate and the median housing value.

And what is this shit about "loan" programs? If the city gets the money for free, how can it be legal to develop a loan program, complete with interest, for poor people and others to have to apply for? Don't you have to have good credit in order to get a loan? For that matter, in Omaha, you have to have good credit in order to get your roof fixed or home renovated. The fact is, if the poor had good credit, they wouldn't need these bullshit programs in the first place, would they?

The Mayor asks and then explains his view, thusly:

> Without this funding, how could all of this be accomplished? We must remember that the dollars that go to the federal government are dollars that come from our residents. This is merely returning some of those dollars back to communities like Lewiston, which desperately need those funds to invest back in our local communities.

All of what? Are the lives of poor people any better off because of the CDBG allocations in Lewiston. Are there less crimes being committed or more minority businesses? Is there a business incubator for the low income? Is the median housing value or the average family income any higher? What was mentioned is good, but they are social service programs, not profits, and nonprofit building structures eat away at the local tax base – that is why they are called "tax-exempt." Then, when you add the tendency of these cities to use "tax incremental financing" for new programs, that erodes the tax base of the low income area all the more. So the rich get richer, the buildings get taller, the downtown sky line improves, the suburbs become more expansive and the ghetto and barrio that generated the grants in the first place, remain as they are or get worse.

"Investing back in our communities" means investing in downtown and mid town, and the suburbs, as is the case in Omaha. It means more places for white people to frolic and have a good time. It means more jobs for white people downtown and beyond. All this is taking place while the poor watch in shock and amazement as their part of the "community" that is supposed to be invested in, becomes increasingly isolated and segregated.

Recalling that this article/letter was penned in early 2011 (February), take note of how fearful these money-grubbers became:

> The U.S. House Republican Study Committee, which is comprised of 175 Representatives, has proposed the total elimination of CDBG. The Obama Administration's budget proposal, according to some sources, may be proposing a cut of up to 25 percent for CDBG in the Administration's Budget.

Nobody was going to do anything with the CDBG program as we now know today, in retrospect. It was just a game, a stall tactic. If you bluff long enough or hard enough with the white man's money, you can get just about everything you want. And even if there were cuts, those cuts would be decided upon by the same opportunists who controlled the grant program in the first place. At each local level, at each of the 1,209 recipient sources, the programs that would be cut first would be those that helped people of color the most. Why? Because that is the most expendable group, that's why. The decision makers hide out where they live, which is the suburbs.

But the lies about how much "good" the CDBG program is doing just keep on coming. But it depends on whose side you're on when the term "good job" is used: the poor are not benefitting from a program that was generated based on the needs of the impoverished. Meanwhile, white folks seem to be having a field day with the program and don't want to see it cut. As the Mayor wrote,

> The entire CDBG budget amounts to close to $4 billion. That amounts to about two weeks of war spending we have been doing for some 10 years now. In light of that spending, CDBG dollars are miniscule. As previously mentioned, every dollar expended in CDBG funding leverages $1.62 in non-CDBG funding. We truly have to view these funds as investment in our local communities. CDBG Grant Funding has been very successful for some 36 years. Why would we want to eliminate or cut a program that has proven to be very successful and of great benefit?

A program can be "successful" and "of great benefit" and still not do what it is supposed to be doing. For instance, the American educational system. Is there any doubt that its successful and of great benefit – to white folks and those who get a decent education at the middle and secondary levels. But is it doing its job in graduating those who are most in need? Of course not. It is successful for those who the system prioritizes – white folks. It's the same way with the CDBG when it comes to local expenditures: they use the triage approach that the military uses. Save those who can be saved and those most in need, let them wait. In that way, the success rate is higher and you can feel good about yourself at the end of the day.

> President Obama, when he met with representatives of the U.S. Conference of Mayors (USCM) recently said: "We also recognize how central cities are to our economy." That is so true. Mr. President and members of Congress, cities and in particular service centers are of critical importance to our economy. This is where taxpayers live and their tax dollars need to be reinvested in the cities that desperately need these funds.

This guy is taking what President Obama said and is mis-interpreting it. What in the FUCK does Obama's reference to "central cities" have to do with CDBG, especially the way that people like Mayor Gilbert have been spending it? Gilbert and his mayoral counterparts AVOID the central city, so why would he be kissing Obama's ass because of a statement that simply acknowledges the existence of these areas?

What "service centers" are so critical to the economy that they get funding from CDBG funds? There are service centers that are critical to black people and brown people, but these groups are ignored and abused by the economy – that does not mean that they are viable parts of it! Gilbert has the nerve to mention where "taxpayers live" and that "their tax dollars need to be reinvested in the cities that desperately need these funds."

What the hell is Mayor Gilbert talking about? The CDBG funding that the cities are already abusing are made up of taxpayers' dollars! Now he wants more of it? These greedy bastards are playing with house money and have shown their disdain for taxpayers, especially minority taxpayers, by the spending decisions they've made.

The pity party for Lewiston continues below:

> Municipalities like Lewiston are at the end of the road. We have federal and state unfunded mandates that are imposed on us. States have been balancing their budgets on the backs of municipalities, such as has happened here when state revenue sharing is cut so the state legislatures can say they have balanced their budgets without raising taxes.

So when these decision makers actually have to put in some work, actually have to do some projections and calculating, all of a sudden being a "leader" becomes an arduous task. But when they're spending and feeding off the teet of the government, that's when they're happiest. These greedy white men are not victims; they are an oppressive force that abuses funding that is supposed to be uplifting low-income people and minorities. It is not until the free money is cut, or threatened to be cut, that all of a sudden these decision makers develop a "conscience."

Mayor Gilbert adds that,

> This only adds to the problem that municipalities have to face by having to lay off valued employees and to moderately increase property taxes on its residents in order to balance its budgets. This regressive tax only hurts those least able to afford them, such as our senior citizens who have worked hard to build their homes and pay their taxes only to find that in their senior years they can no longer afford to keep their homes.

The Mayor is leaving out an important fact: senior citizens paid into the system and they are getting back what they've paid in. In like manner, black people have paid into this system with our blood, sweat and tears and all these people want to do is rip us off time and time again. Everybody is going to eventually get old, so that is a category that those in power care about; but if you isolate and segregate people of color good enough, you don't even have to see them, let alone care about applying money to upgrade their collective condition.

Furthermore,

> As mayors throughout the country, we are not asking for an
> increase in CDBG funding, but merely asking the President
> and Congress to maintain the $4 billion 2010 level for both
> the current fiscal year (2011) and the next fiscal year (2012).
> I quote from a communiqué by the USCM: "CDBG funding
> does not stay in city hall. It goes to thousands of local
> businesses, contractors and service providers."

The fact of the matter is, people like Mayor Gilbert have a lot of gall to be asking for anything as it relates to CDBG. The collective track record of these local decision makers and their planning departments has continued to spit in the face of the people who the grant was supposed to serve. Has unemployment among African-Americans decreased? No. Has affordable housing in the black community increased? Barely. With more than $4 billion having been spent in 2010, you would think that these cities would be a lot better off today than they were when the CDBG grant first started in the late 1970s. Are they? No.

Poverty is on the rise, as is crime. Unemployment among black people is continuing to be sky high and jobs are leaving these cities despite their spending CDBG money on incentives and tax breaks to try to keep these businesses. Even when they bring businesses in, there is no guarantee that any one of them is going to hire any people of color. The black communities are being ignored for the most part, but for those who have some potential CDBG money is being used to parcel them out and sell bits and pieces, especially if those areas are anywhere near a riverfront that they can transform into an area of leisure or a downtown where they can feed off of the location and change the skyline. Black people, for the most part, are not included in any of this. Even the work taking place WITHIN black communities is farmed out to white developers who, in turn, don't want to hire black people.

Quoting from some national source, Mayor Gilbert comments that, "CDBG funding does not stay in city hall. It goes to thousands of local businesses, contractors and service providers." If this statement was broken down by race and class, we would find that those "thousands" would be overwhelmingly white, would be people who may hunker down in low income areas but who do not live among the masses, and people who are upper middle class and therefore do not have any serious concern about the low-income people whose negative demographics qualified these cities for the grant in the first place.

When in doubt and you need minority input, just call on the largest black church in the area (or churches if there is more than one) and get them to sell out and co-sign on what the city is doing. These ministers will do anything in order to get that envelope of money under the table, and if they have to sell out their own congregation, so be it. Being excellent speakers, they will do their damndest to convince black people that the white man is our friend and has our best interests at heart. And, like the sheep that the term "flock" implies that they are, they follow their preacher like willing thralls.

That is why Mayor Gilbert writes the following:

> I now call upon our faith community, who truly see the value
> of the social services that these funds help to provide, to
> contact our congressional delegation to support the effort to
> maintain this level of CDBG funding.

Why should it take the so called "faith community" to "truly see the value of social services"? I'll tell you why: because the faith community that he's talking about is black, and because of racism and discrimination, the people who need those services the most are ALSO African-American. Just like the white man was able to get some Uncle Tom-Tom Indians to help him, just like today sell out black politicians curry favor with and do the bidding of their former slave master, that is what Mayor Gilbert is talking about: get the people who are most likely to side with us, who can be bought off, and who less likely to give a shit about the end result. This describes most ministers to a "t."

Many of these poverty pimps benefited from the CDBG allocations, getting small payoffs for pet projects like senior housing, day care centers, paved parking lots and so on. Most ministers have an "edifice complex" – they compete among themselves on who has the most successful capital campaigns for expansion, who has the most impressive church façade or the most beautiful building. That's what they do. They sell the ignorant a line of bullshit about pie-in-the-sky while the white man gets his "heaven" right here on earth, right NOW!

After addressing the need to call on "de cullud folk," Mayor Gilbert then has a role for the legitimate capitalists:

> I call upon the local business community, members of the
> Chamber of Commerce, contractors who see the value in
> infrastructure investments and with their strong voice to assist
> in this effort to protect these critical services so as to not
> negatively impact the business climate of our city.

In other words, he's calling on these entities to take the proactive role that they abandoned when they saw the "free money" coming down the pike! They got lax and took their resources and money and got selfish. Now, with the money being threatened, the Mayor is warning them that things might get rough, so do your jobs! If these were black people or people of color running these programs or operating as a mayor and making such a plea, they would be run out of town on a rail the way that Kwame Kilpatrick (rightfully) was in Detroit.

The article's conclusion rings as hollow as most of what this Mayor had to say about CDBG and its application in Lewiston and nationally:

> If we were to look back over the past 36 years without CDBG
> funding, we would be aghast as to what we may take for
> granted today that would otherwise not have been realized.
> Please do as I have: contact our congressional delegation
> today. Thank you in advance for supporting your community.

What Mayor Gilbert has to learn is that when it comes to the black community, we CAN look back over the past 36 years and see what has taken place. Our communities have gotten worse while other parts of the city, using money that was generated by OUR poverty, is spread downtown, in the suburbs and to hire people who do not look like us or live where we live. When "negroes" are employed, they are hired solely to do the bidding of the planning departments and to ignore the basic housing and employment needs of other black people.

Who is the "we" who is taking the CDBG allocations for granted? It's the various city administrations and their planning departments. It's the people who have benefited and the nonprofit white-run programs that perpetuate poverty while at the same time making sure that they keep their jobs long enough to make that mortgage payment and car note. This is taking place all over the nation in the top cities receiving CDBG, and in the next section of this paper, I share with you the allocations of two cities: Omaha and Milwaukee. Both corrupt, both continually making decisions that only serve to further isolate and alienate the black community, and both as racially segregated today in 2014 as they were in 1975.

NEBRASKA'S PLEA TO KEEP CDBG

On July 8, 2012, a year and four months after the previous article and information was appearing around the rest of the nation, *The Omaha World Herald* issues an editorial titled, "Don't Mess With Success." I am about to share the contents of that editorial with you to show how CDBG works in Nebraska, which is a unique situation because it is a large state physically but has a very meager population. It shows how they will beg and plead for more money for their cities but when black people were getting welfare, it was looked down upon as "leeching."

On July 8, 2012 the *World Herald* published an editorial titled, "Don't Mess With Success." I am about to share the contents of that editorial with you to show, not only how CDBG works in Nebraska, but how the same thing is taking place in mid-sized Milwaukee and mega-sized Dallas. The following article is filled with half-truths, false research findings, grandiose claims, hyperbole and, you guessed it: bullshit.

Check it out for yourself:

> From one end of the state to the other, Nebraska communities are benefiting from the Community Development Block Grant program. Through it, cities and towns have loaned federal CDBG funds to many small businesses. An estimated $20 million in such loans currently are in circulation in Nebraska, and no one has stepped forward to say they have worked out badly. In fact, when asked by World-Herald reporter Paul Hammel, a federal official emphasized there was no information to suggest that cities had used the money inappropriately.

When these white people found out that the Community Development Block Grant funds might be drying up, the newspapers across the nation, as a collective starting running editorials similar to the one you are reading from the Omaha World Herald. I have found similar editorials in the Dallas Morning News, the Denver Post, the Los Angeles Times, the New York Times, the Detroit Free Press and the Cincinnati Post. They may have sound arguments as to why the funds should not be cut off in their major cities (although I doubt it, since all applicants have to rely on black and Latino poverty to even qualify).

But Omaha and Nebraska do not have that right.

Creating a loan program out of free money is highly unethical and I made this a key point of my injunction that I filed back in 1995. A loan, as anyone will tell you, is the first step back into slavery. You have to pay that money back, with interest, and the criteria are as steep as any bank. This means that the program makes money from money that they already got for free.

In the previous passage it is stated that a reporter whom I have much respect for, Paul Hammel, asked about the problems with the program, the person answering claimed that "there was no information to suggest that cities had used the money inappropriately.

Either Paul is lying, the World-Herald twisted his words, or both parties have been living under a rock for the past decade. I have pointed out in countless newspaper articles and major white papers that Omaha has abused the CDBG program. I pointed out how they did it, when it started, how much they've received since 1975 (the year of the first grant) and who the key scam artists in the Planning Department were.

I believe that these people were going through their files and came across some of my old writings in the Omaha Star and in my scathing letters to their editorial board. I believe that they are trying to cover their tracks and even more than that, here is a key concern of mine.

How would such information regarding the inappropriate use of CDBG funds be made public? When you submit information to local planning departments, they bury or trash it. When you appear at the Citizens Advisory meetings (which are mandatory but are not promoted, at least not in Omaha), they turn a deaf ear and then point to some of their suburban accomplishments. So when this unnamed federal official (this is a newspaper – why not name who said it, that is, if the person truly exists?) says that "there is no information to suggest" that the cities did anything inappropriately, what he really means is that "there is no information available."

Information is in abundance if these people would just listen to Sen. Inouye of Hawaii. He's made it clear that the CDBG programs around the nation are a mayor's joy and a city's delight: free money every year. I've made this point in Omaha for over 25 years, and they well know it. So when Paul Hammel turns in this kind of comment, it just so happens to "jibe" with what the goal of the editorial is: to absolve Nebraska and its cities of any wrongdoing and to keep the money flowing into the coffers of this hick state.

The editorial continues with the claim that, "On the contrary, the loans have produced real benefits. They've been distributed based on sound management by local governments, and they've helped achieve the goal that our country's leaders, across philosophical and partisan lines, are all rightly pushing: Creating jobs."

Where are the statistics to back up these claims of "sound management"? If these organizations were so "sound," why didn't they go after traditional business loans from a bank or from the Small Business Administration? Why go on the government dole and use CDBG funds? The point is that these major newspapers feel they don't have to prove anything: as long as they print it, then that alone, makes it so. The World-Herald owns almost every newspaper in the state of Nebraska, an unheard of reality. So it is in their best interests to print these half-truths because almost everybody in the state of not even two million people will read it and believe it. Few people will do any research on their own because the key word in CDBG is "grant" – that means free money.

As for creating jobs, where are the figures? How many? If the employment figures are so profound and the management so sound, then share the information with us on a city-by-city basis. Talking about "creating jobs" by a politician is nothing more than an essential necessity: the question is, are any of them doing it? Nebraska already had one of the lowest unemployment rates in the nation, so how are we going to tell if progress has been made unless we do a comparative analysis of some kind, or perhaps a cluster sample of small businesses across the state. Maybe even a survey. But that would be too much work and it might not generate the kinds of "conclusions" that the editorial is looking for. So they just keep it generic and vanilla enough to get across a central point to the feds: "Boss, don't take away our gravy train"!

Continuing:

> A recent World-Herald news article noted the specific examples in Pawnee City. There, the funds have helped a pet food factory with 130 employees as well as a winery and brewery. CDBG loans helped provide funds for new storefronts at five businesses. Since the 1980s, the article noted, "the Pawnee City Revolving Loan Fund has helped create or retain dozens of jobs — and has never lost a cent on a loan." Such economic development provides a significant boost to a community like Pawnee City, with a population of 878. And yet, the rug has been pulled out from under the program.

Why specifically Pawnee City? What will one so-called "success story"? If there is all the blanket production that the editorial claims there is, why not use a bulleted list of various cities? If the rug has been pulled from under Pawnee City, then it is for a sound business reason: the government is not going to risk a law suit. If there are only 878 people in the city, what kind of progress could be expected? And how could any progress be deemed a "significant boost" in a city that doesn't even have a thousand people in it? If these businesses have the wherewithal to pay back those loans – with interest -- then they can muster up enough money to hire employees on their own.

Here comes the place where they pit "ideal" against "reality:"

> The federal Department of Housing and Urban Development now says all CDBG loans must be rigorously scrutinized for total compliance with federal requirements on matters such as environmental issues and prevailing-wage rules. The current approach — by which Nebraska cities and towns file a compliance report every six months with the state — is no longer good enough, HUD claims. Omaha, Lincoln and Bellevue are too large to be affected, but dozens of towns across Nebraska are directly impacted.

Weren't those loans already being "rigorously scrutinized"? And if they weren't then why not? And if they had to upgrade and begin to pay attention, how much was lost during that period? What does rigorously scrutinized for total compliance mean? Does that mean that people were getting loans and were only *partially* in compliance? In my injunction I proposed that these people be forced to submit compliance reports on a BI- MONTHLY (every two months) basis because there is too much money at stake to settle for anything less.

As for those "dozens of towns across Nebraska" that are affected by the new compliance laws, that should be no problem: the smaller the town, the less paperwork and therefore the easier it should be to "comply," right?

Here are more lies that make me believe that somebody got ahold of one of my previous reports:

> The feds say the stepped-up compliance is required under a 1992 law governing the CDBG program. Yet no one is offering a reasonable explanation about why Nebraska communities only now are being clobbered with this new enforcement requirement even though the law went on the books 20 years ago. The situation has led the state Department of Economic Development (DED) to tell Nebraska communities it would be best if they turn over the current unloaned CDBG money — estimated at $8 million — to the state so it can be distributed through new, regional entities.

What was going on prior to 1992? That's why Senator Inouye, myself and others are pointing out the waste that is taking place by these "trial and error" administrators who view the CDBG program as a "free meal ticket."

Now another lie where Hammel writes, " … no one is offering a reasonable explanation about why Nebraska communities only now are being clobbered with this new enforcement requirement even though the law went on the books 20 years ago." To begin with, I pointed out a plethora of violations and improprieties on the part of the Omaha program. Secondly, if the law went on the books 20 years ago what difference does it make if there is a "new enforcement"? The fact is, the law should have been followed, plain and simple.

But this proves the point. If there is no monitoring, these states will go crazy over that money and cities like Omaha, that receive the lion's share, will do whatever they want because there is no one checking on them to ensure compliance. They have to be watched in order to do the right thing, especially when it comes to minority allocations. Why weren't the demographics of these loans and the grant allocations that are also a part of the CDBG allocation process, also shared with the public?

Next comes the threat of penalty:

> One possible penalty for failing to meet federal regulations, the department said in one message, would be to block a community from receiving any new CDBG money for two

years. A lot of Nebraska community leaders, plus officials at
the Nebraska League of Municipalities, have understandably
expressed exasperation, or worse, at this turn of events.

They express exasperation when a proposed penalty would take away their free government money, but they had no problem threatening to do the same thing to food stamp recipients, Section 8 recipients, welfare recipients and even social security disability recipients who didn't "tow the line." And these entities were cruel about it as well. Senator Inouye stated on television that the one program that these major cities would not want to lose is the CDBG program, and that is because it's free money and there's a lot of discretion involved with it; in other words, city planners and others can pretty much do whatever they want to do with it, even though the grants are generated based on black and Latino poverty-related demographics.

According to the *Omaha World Herald* editorial,

> Last week, the DED told Nebraska cities that it's placing a 60-day pause on this issue to give the state and municipalities time to explore options. That's prudent. A deep breath is needed right now. Fewer than 10 cities have decided to turn their funds over to the state, and the DED says they will have the chance to reconsider that step. Seventy-five Nebraska municipalities have sought an extension on whether to hand over their funds.

Begging for extensions just like the Mayor of Lewiston was doing earlier. Breathing a collective sigh of relief. Now they know how they make people of color and low-income whites feel when they – the CDBG Administrators and their gatekeepers – "lay down the law" and put pressure on low income individuals, families and neighborhoods. These CDBG Administrators have been getting away with abuse for decades. In the case of Omaha, since 1975, more than $276 million dollars has come through the city, money that was supposed to be going toward fixing up North Omaha, providing jobs for the residents and the like. Today, in 2012, North Omaha's streets, lights, and sewers look worse than they did in 1977.

Continuing:

> No one disputes that monitoring always is needed to guard against inappropriate use of taxpayer funds. But all indications are that, as a whole, local governments in Nebraska have been managing the CDBG loans responsibly. It makes no sense that a program with such practical successes should be sidetracked and burdened by this remarkable eruption of stepped-up

regulations, miscommunication and uncertainty. The
appropriate response should include a large dose of leadership
and common sense.

All indications are that as a whole, local governments in Nebraska have been managing the CDBG loans responsibly? What are these indications? Why not list them? Since we're talking about monitoring, there must be an evaluation or assessment methodology that can be shared with the public so that we, the people, can see for ourselves if those loans have been managed "responsibly" or not. And what about the state level allocations of the CDBG: are they managing *their* roles in regard to the loans, responsibly? In terms of disbursement, are they handling things correctly or perhaps, skimming off the top?

After creating a straw man that consists of the (false) belief that things are on the up-and-up, the article builds on that claim by stating that because of the responsible management, it therefore "makes no sense that a program with such practical successes should be sidetracked and burdened by this remarkable eruption of stepped-up regulations, miscommunication and uncertainty." Remarkable eruption? If all is going along as smoothly as the World-Herald claims, then there would be no eruption – perhaps a small glitch or a little bump in the road. There would only be a "remarkable eruption" if something were sorely amiss, if there was a major problem of some kind.

And look at what these newspaper editors view as "remarkable eruptions:" stepped-up regulations, miscommunication and uncertainty. To begin with, any organization or agency should have enough foresight to expect regulatory changes from time to time. *Only the ones that aren't managed well would consider such changes as a "remarkable eruption."* Secondly, what "miscommunication"? It seems that this entire episode is the prototype for excellent governmental communication. It's clear that these cities got the message loud and clear! If there is any miscommunication, cite some examples of it. Was the source of it the government or the cities impacted? Inquiring minds want to know!

And finally, the claim of "uncertainty." What is uncertain about what has been written? If the writing is on the wall, then the time spent writing editorials could better be spent finding out the source of the uncertainty. How can the World-Herald make the claim that all is fine in Nebraska under a cloud of that which they then deem as being "uncertain"? Clearly, the World-Herald piece is an article written to beg the government to back off because the businesses that succeed in these cities have to advertise, and since the World-Herald owns almost every newspaper in the entire state, they have a financial stake in writing editorials claiming that "all is well."

Then the methods of operation to "resolve" the issue are shared. I'm glad. The same people at these meetings will be receiving copies of a white paper I am preparing, which includes the perennial abuse of the CDBG program by the city of Omaha. It won't be the first one that I've sent them.

At any rate, the editorial clams that, "First, Nebraska community officials will be meeting with HUD on this matter. They'll be doing the same with the state DED. That's good. But those meetings need to produce results. The participants need to explore all options for sensible flexibility on this issue."

The state Department of Economic Development should have been involved in the first place. This is the area where there might be some "mismanagement," since they are in charge of dealing with the economic realities of the entire state. The "Nebraska officials" that will be meeting with HUD are going to do nothing but sing the same praise songs that the World Herald did; they know they have a hick state that only has two cities with over 100,00 people (Omaha and Lincoln), and they know that every sent that they can scrounge up helps to keep more people from packing up and leaving. Tourism is a joke because Nebraska is not a destination state: *people drive through here heading to someplace else.*

After stating the obvious – that being that the meetings "need to produce results" (hence, "meetings"), the brain surgeons at the Omaha World Herald add that, "the participants need to explore all options for sensible flexibility on this issue." Sensible flexibility? In other words, "exceptions," "waivers," "conditional probation"? They want mercy, slack and understanding when it is their asses on the line; but remember how they (the state) treated the welfare recipients and the black child care owners, in the state's largest black community in Omaha? It seems to be a case of "different strokes for different folks."

Who are these "officials" that will be meeting with HUD? Well among them will be members of Congress: "Second, Nebraska's congressional delegation should make clear both to HUD and to their fellow lawmakers that Congress needs to look closely at the 1992 law and HUD's belated follow-up regulations. If sensible adjustments are warranted, make them."

Who is Nebraska going to "make it clear to"? They'd better be in there asking questions and eating humble pie! These Congressmen will be the ones begging for allocations come budget time, so they'd better tip lightly! As for HUDs allegedly "belated" regulations, that's a lie: the editorial just said that the information had been on the books 20 years. If anything is "belated" it is Nebraska's reaction to what has taken place and the fact that their elected officials were too backward to see the writing on the wall and prepare these various towns and cities for the impending changes!

The editorial notes, "If sensible adjustments are warranted, make them." Who are they to define what is "sensible" and what is not? The rules are there in black and white. And the government is a fickle beast to begin with, dependent on so many people to agree on so little. So that which is "sensible" is defined by those who have the money, not by those who need it! If that was the case, the CDBG wouldn't be overlooking black communities all over the nation when it came to doling out money for anything other than small-time arts projects and "negro organizations" that they (these cities) control!

Playing the role of the "unwitting victim," the World-Herald, speaking for those who have been allegedly "negatively impacted," concludes the article, thusly:

> Third, this controversy has strained the DED's relations with some community leaders as well as the Nebraska League of Municipalities. All parties need to work on turning things around, nurturing good communication and rebuilding trust. This is a case where government has needlessly thrown a wrench in the gears of a program that was working well. So much angst and confusion could have been avoided had government heeded a common-sense lesson: Don't mess with success.

If this "controversy" strained the Department of Economic Development's relationship with "some community leaders," who cares? Those so-called community leaders need DED, not vice-versa. And as for the so-called Nebraska League of Municipalities, how powerful can they be: the entire state has 1.8 million people in it, and yet it's the fifth largest in terms of overall land mass. In simple terms, it's country once you get outside of Lincoln, so the so called League is probably Omaha-heavy with input and control. As they say in the vernacular of the ghetto, "you got to bring ass to get ass."

Then comes the general, philosophical, ethical advice: "All parties need to work on turning things around, nurturing good communication and rebuilding trust." This is advice that the World-Herald, which works toward choosing leadership in black communities, defending mis-allocations of funds and even went so far as to get involved in an election by giving a mayoral candidate a blind lie-detector test, should take itself. It is one of the most unethical papers in the nation and always has been. Simply read the *Columbia Journalism Review* "cheers and jeers" section and you'll see what I mean.

After a quick poke at ethical reform, the article gets back to the blame game by stating, "This is a case where government has needlessly thrown a wrench in the gears of a program that was working well." The question is: working well for whom? The plow works well for the farmer who is behind it – but ask the mule who's doing the work how HE feels about it! CDBG money has been manipulated and wasted in Nebraska, especially in Omaha, for over thirty-five years. I've added the City of Milwaukee, ranked 17th nationally in size, to provide a point of comparison that shows that from the small (Omaha is number 41 in size) to the mid-sized, CDBG is shelling out big money and the cities are having a veritable ball spending it. Let me provide a chart that provides an example of what has been doled out by the Feds from 1975 through 1997:

TABLE 1: Distribution of Community Development Block Grants in Milwaukee and Omaha, 1975 to 1997

City/CDBG Recipient	Year of Allocation	CDBG Amount (per $1,000)
Milwaukee	1975-1976	$13,383
Omaha	1975-1976	1,390
Milwaukee	1980-1981	22,794
Omaha	1980-1981	5,912
Milwaukee	1985-1986*	17,684
Omaha	1985-1986	4,833
Milwaukee	1988	25,090
Omaha	1988	3,715
Milwaukee	1989	15,362
Omaha	1989	3,868
Milwaukee	1990	15,328
Omaha	1990	3,654
Milwaukee	1991	14,342
Omaha	1991	3,470
Milwaukee	1992	16,233
Omaha	1992	5,587
Milwaukee	1993	16,101
Omaha	1993	6,409
Milwaukee	1994	20,500
Omaha	1994	7,024
Milwaukee	1995	22,000
Omaha	1995	7,335
Milwaukee	1996	24,274
Omaha	1996	7,056
Milwaukee	1997	24,705
Omaha	1997	6,950
	TOTAL:	*$247,796*

	Milw.	116,748
	Omaha	

***Switched from fiscal year to calendar year.**

Now, simply visit the urban core of these areas. Both of them have Latinos relegated to the South side, and therefore both cities have the required "pocket of poverty." Milwaukee's program has suffered from some well-publicized abuse from City Council members, while Omaha's abuse mainly stems from decisions made by a lily-white Planning Department, which recently hired a black man from out of state to serve as its director. Now, according to their warped thinking (like those who think that America is no longer racist now that there's a black president), charges of racial discrimination in allocations, past or present, become null-and-void.

I don't think this is a case where "government has needlessly thrown a wrench in the gears of a program that was working well." I think its better late than never! Look at those numbers I just showed you: where in the world has $116,000,000 gone? And remember, this is only through 1997 – 15 years ago. *So there has easily been $200 million ploughed into Omaha coffers alone since 1975.* Again, visit the black and Latino communities that constitute the "pocket of poverty." In neither of these cities is there a "white pocket of poverty." Do you think this is an accident or a quirk?

Then, with arrogance that is typical of a paper that has a monopoly over the thinking of an entire state, the editorial concludes: "So much angst and confusion could have been avoided had government heeded a common-sense lesson: Don't mess with success."

"Success," *Omaha World Herald*, is defined by those who provide the money. If the government feels that something is wrong, they would be wasting money, energy and time "investigating" and "correcting" that which is already functioning. This is all about advertising revenue and keeping the cities enriched with money so that the businesses that need that money can stay afloat and place their promotions, want-ads, employee of the week articles, *and other paid print information* in one of the World-Herald's many newspapers.

THE CITY OF OMAHA'S ABUSE OF CDBG

The abuse of CDBG funds and other Federal monies by the city of Omaha has a long history, and the kinds of "tactics" used included the assistance of certain "negro leaders" who were brought in to do the bidding of the city administration.

In the first scenario, I go back to 1980-81, where the city created and then enlisted a "pseudo development" group of blacks called NOCD and how, after this, even the police chief went after some of the CDBG monies. In both instances, the black community of Omaha in general and the 68111 zip code – the poorest of the poor within that milieu -- was ignored.

In the second, I provide a chart of the 1993-94 grant allocations and clearly show how the 68111 zip code is totally ignored.

In the first instance, the group called "North Omaha Community Development" (an oxymoron) and their statement. From their own prospectus they offered the following:

> The first incorporation of an organization named North Omaha Community Development was in 1972. It was an outgrowth of a grant received by the City of Omaha from the United States Department of Housing and Urban Development (H.U.D.). The objective of the grant was to prepare a community development plan ... Pursuant (sic) to a provision in the grant for citizen participation, the City made an effort to insure resident input ... Eventually a group emerged from this City initiated effort and incorporated as North Omaha Community Development .... " (NOCD, no date)

The community development plan that included "NOCD" was a joke, and was written by the decision makers and some hand picked "negroes" that would do their bidding. To ensure that they would, NOCD was placed on the CDBG payroll and under the control of the city's orders and plans. While fronting as being "pro-community," NOCD was really nothing more than a façade, a sort of "outpost" in the black community.

After several years of paving the way for the city of encroach on North Omaha (with the help of Omaha Economic Development Corporation and several other "shills") in in around 1979 the city found a "negro" with a bachelor's degree from Yale University. They then proudly marched out George Garnett, and made him the "director" of the organization, and the media jumped on it, making the arrival of this man would finally turn North Omaha's neighborhoods around. At one point Garnett told the major newspaper, "Traditionally, 24th and Lake has been the center of business, the spiritual center of the community. If that area can be revitalized, it will have a ripple effect and it will be easier to turn the rest of the community around." (Omaha World Herald, no date)

The central city apparently trusted both the city administration and NOCD. After all, in the same article, written by the Omaha World Herald's only black reporter, Sibyl Myers, it was "predicted" that,

> In the next six months to a year, there will be a marked change in the appearance of North Omaha, the new executive director of North Omaha Community Development Inc. said. And in five years, North Omaha will have 'a new facelift that not only will make the area more viable but also will make people not recognize it," George Garnett said.

That was more than thirty years ago. The only thing that was "visible" was a black fence that encircled what is now the Technology and Business Center, and it was such a stupid idea that Senator Ernie Chambers was able to embarrass the city into taking it down. Once again, central city residents' trust had been betrayed. Here in 2014, with NOCD having failed miserably and having disbanded, the area looks worse now than it did back in the late seventies-early 1980s.

In 1981, a group called the Real Estate Research Corporation was bought in from outside and made even more promises. These were designed to give NOCD credibility and to make it appear as if the city's planners really cared about North Omaha. In shaky language, part of the report stated,

> "At the corner of 24th and Lake Streets, the "Blue Lion Center" should become the cornerstone of efforts to rehabilitate the North Omaha business district .... The new center is intended to be the catalyst for commercial redevelopment in the area ... New businesses will be sought to move into the center, and existing nearby businesses will be encouraged to remodel their own buildings ..." (King, 1981: 6)

The Blue Lion Centre was up and running and is probably, at best, breaking even. The few businesses that it was able to attract failed and nothing even close to "commercial development" was developed. What existing businesses? What was written above appeared thirty three years ago. Today the 24th and Lake Street area is all but abandoned, and the city of Omaha owns all four corners of the once popular cultural jazz section. There is no real commercial development. A "negro" named Michael Maroney has taken over the so called Omaha Economic Development Corporation (a modern day NOCD) and has built houses that can't be rented and office space that goes on un –used. All this in preparation for the return of whites to the inner city, which is right next to riverfront development and downtown. In the meantime, blacks are being relocated to the northwestern sector of the city.

To add insult to injury, an *Omaha World Herald* editorial, titled "North Omaha Sky Brightens," continued to promise jobs to the area as has always been the case:

> "Last August, it was noted editorially that there was a surge of activity to revitalize Omaha's North Side ... Omaha also appears finally ready to get on with building the extension of the North Freeway and the Arthur C. Storz Expressway to Eppley Airfield. This should offer the better transportation needed to provide development and jobs in the area. As the new year begins, the skies over North Omaha do, indeed, look brighter for 1981 and the years to follow." (Omaha World Herald, 1981: 4)

Again, some 33 years after the publication of this statement, the only reality is the North Freeway, which was really built to expedite the trip from west Omaha suburbs to the airport. Where is the "better transportation" for those who live in North Omaha? Where is the development? Where are the jobs? So, aiding and abetting the city planning department and local politicians, the Omaha World Herald *lied* when it wrote, "as the new year begins, the skies over North Omaha do, indeed look brighter for 1981 and the years to follow."

The productive structure that came out of all those years and work is the Blue Lion Center which as of August 2014 sits abandoned. On the southwest side is Family Housing Assistance Services, which is hardly even used. On the north western side is the Love Jazz Center, space rental that is hardly ever used and which failed when the handpicked director took the money and ran. On the north eastern side is a minority business incubator that has done little for minority development (except for their friends) and that is in violation of the rules of any quality business incubator in existence. Instead of providing minority businesses with a place to start out and learn about business and then get out into the real world and apply it, there are black businesses in that place that have been sitting in there over twenty years, while the City charges them rent.

All the rest of the Community Development Block Grant money went to the city administration, white contractors and some "negroes" that Senator Chambers exposed in a January 1982 response to North Omaha Community Development:

> From Marty Shukert [then the planning director for the City ... came information establishing a heavy financial tie justifying the characterization of NOCD as an **adjunct** to the city. Since 1977, the city has funneled loans and grants to NOCD totaling

$2,046,936. Of that amount, $32,127 was a **grant** to
rehabilitate the NOCD building owned by NOCD president
Carl Tyler. Another $114,000 in grants went primarily for
NOCD salaries. As a **moneyless** "co-developer" of the Garden
Apartments, and a shill for Greater Omaha Corporation, NOCD
received a grant of $850,000 and a loan of $300,000 at 3
percent, and a share of the title..." (Chambers, 1982: 33--
emphasis original)

And,

As the **moneyless** sole developer of the Blue Lion Project at
24th and Lake, the NOCD will receive a grant of $400,000 and
a **loan** of $300,000 and the title." (Chambers, 1982 p. 33).

NOCD is now gone, and the building is deteriorating as quickly as the
immediate community surrounding it. More lies and more tricks. All aimed at
pacifying the black community while the millions that this community generates --
through its poverty, high unemployment, older houses and overall blighted
condition -- is spent elsewhere, primarily downtown and in areas which are faring
much better.

And the tricks continued, all aimed at cutting huge chunks out of the CDBG
money and, of course, neglect North Omaha

In March of 1982, seven years after the CDBG Program began in Omaha
and a year when the city would receive $5,842,000, a 12-member committee was
formed to study revitalization and crime in the 24th and Lake Street area, with the
first meeting being held at then Mayor Mike Boyle's office. Further,

Police Chief Robert Wadman said the committee, which
also includes eight members active in North Omaha
Community Development Inc., will discuss ways in which
police can help the rebuilding of deteriorated North Omaha
areas..." (Omaha World Herald, 1982: p. 4)

Now, the money factor:

With the aid of about $800,000 in Community
Development Block Grant money, that intersection
currently is undergoing a facelift, including landscaping
and renovation of two vacant buildings into specialty
shops, entertainment facilities and office space..." (Omaha
World Herald, 1982: p. 4)

What "entertainment facilities" were supposed to be built or created? Where are they? Here in 2014, none exist within North Omaha. And any that open up along Ames Avenues have been closed by the City Council allegedly due to mismanagement and criminal activity taking place outside of those facilities. More promises, abuse of monies brought to the city because of the "pocket of poverty" which the near Northside represents, and very little happens except that outside interests (read: "white"), architects, planners, heavy equipment manufacturers, construction workers and of course, politicians (through re-election), get rich.

<u>The Impact of CDBG Cuts on the North Side</u>

An article titled, "CDBG Takes Another Hit," which appeared in the March 2012 edition of a planning journal titled, Governing, included the following statement:

> Because local governments' revenue still hasn't returned to pre-recession levels, most local leaders say they can't substitute their own funds for the amount cut by the feds. "It's forcing us and a lot of other communities to start making very hard choices," says Eric Brown, director of housing and community development for Prince George's County, Md., which saw its CDBG funds cut by about 23 percent to $4.2 million this year. "We're looking at what our priorities are and trying to make do with the limited resources we have to fund those priorities." (Holeywell, 2012).

Omaha has known for some time that the Community Development Block Grant money was going to dry up. The late senator Daniel Inouye of Hawaii exposed the abuse that was taking place, and I sent him several documents showing how Omaha was abusing the money and not putting it in the black community, an area whose poverty enabled them to qualify for the money in the first place.

Today, in 2014, Omaha ranks number one in the nation in black child poverty, and number one in the nation in black on black youth homicide. Both of these may sound like social problems, but they are actually the result of financial decisions made by the City of Omaha for the past three decades. The plan is to maintain its "pocket of poverty" (ghetto) so that they can keep qualifying for CDBG funding. In doing so, the negative conditions remain the same or grow worse, and by documenting the problems, the City can obtain even larger grants as time goes on. The key is to PRETEND as if you care about North Omaha when, in reality, all that is being done is relocating it to the northwest, stealing the money that its poverty generates, and use that money to develop other parts of the city.

Keep North Omaha poor. That is why there are so many nonprofits in the area. Nonprofit means "tax exempt' meaning no taxes are paid on the organizations or the buildings. How can you maintain a community with no taxes being generated? The City of Omaha has 458 total churches and of that number 116 of them are in North Omaha. Add to those nonprofits the presence of the Boys Club, North Point, the YMCA and scores of smaller nonprofits, and the area is broke, for the short-term and for the future.

After that, take that impoverished status and put it in an application for Federal grant assistance, pledging to "help." Then when the money comes, forget all about that promise and go on about your business and allow North Omaha to wither away like the last leaves of a painfully prolonged autumn.

In April of 2014 I filed a $200 million grievance against the City of Omaha and its abuse of CDBG money. I am still working on and preparing for my confrontation with them (not the first) and hope to at very least expose them for their criminal behavior toward the black community – maybe even coerce and apology from their lying mouths.

<u>$200 Million Lawsuit Filed Against City: Stelly v. City of Omaha</u>

Following is a copy of a letter to the community that I submitted to the Omaha Star newspaper (the only black newspaper in Nebraska) for publication in August of 2014. Will they print it? Who knows. But here it is, in its entirety, a letter outlining the thrust of my nearly 60 page brief against the City of Omaha:

The following article does not represent the views of the Omaha Star newspaper or its staff. Neighborhood Association Seeks Relief from HUD for North Omaha's CDBG $$$$$

Since 1975, the City of Omaha has received more than $210 million dollars from the federal government through the Community Development Block Grant program to upgrade North Omaha in the area of jobs, housing, social welfare and street upgrades. Councilman Ben Gray's recent demand for roads to be fixed echoes a similar demand that Triple One, along with several churches including Gould Ministries, made more than 20 years ago, replete with videotapes of poor sidewalks, potholes, dilapidated housing and other community needs.
Nothing was done.

Because of North Omaha's poverty, the City continues to send in grant after grant to the government asking for money that will "make things better." These requests include Community Service Block Grants, Weed and Seed Grants and many others. Once the money arrives, the City or recipient gets "selective amnesia" and spends the money out west, downtown or on some form of leisure like they did when they build Eugene Leahy Park and the downtown skyline.

A full copy of our 58 page grievance was mailed out in April to the Department of Housing and Urban Development (HUD), the Office of the Inspector General, and other appropriate CDBG-related entities to expose the chicanery taking place in the city of Omaha by its Planning Department. It appears that these Federal 'oversight" agencies and related entities are complicit in this 39 year record of discrimination by the City of Omaha Planning Department who never, during this period, had good intentions in terms of allocation of monies that would alleviate the very poverty in North Omaha that qualified the city proper for these grants in the first place. While local colleges receive federal money for "neighborhood centers" and build "community engagement centers" on campus, there is little serious impact on the community whose poverty stats they pimp in order to qualify for the money in the first place.

We will spread the word. In the meantime, be reminded of the following excerpt from our original grievance:

- Under the Program Fraud Civil Remedy Act, we demand that the Office of the Inspector General charge the City of Omaha with abuse of Federal funds and our suit demands civil monetary penalties in the amount of $200 million, the approximate amount that the City has accepted from the Federal government only to steer these funds to other parts of the city as well as the coffers of city employers, former members of the Planning Department, junkets and the construction industry.
- In an area of the city with the highest unemployment rate in the nation, no black contractors are involved in street projects and CDBG will hire none of them despite the fact that 16 members of the Planning Department staff are paid out of CDBG funds. In addition four former Planning leaders now get paid as "consultants" and one of them is directing the city's largest
- Through diligent documentation of black poverty, unemployment, dilapidated housing, drug abuse, violent crime and so on, Omaha bought attention to its "pocket of poverty," received more than $200 million in free money since 1975, and proceeded to ignore the very area of the city whose poverty generated those grant funds in the first place (explained in greater chronological detail elsewhere in this document. Ask yourself: does North Omaha look better and are its residents faring better than they did in 1975?

The Inspector General Act of 1978 made it clear that the priority over CDBG and other HUD programs was the promotion of "efficiency and effectiveness" in programs and operations. Omaha's City Planning Department did neither, but instead, padded its own coffers, hired unqualified individuals (with black tokenism added) and went on a veritable shopping spree using Federal dollars and ignoring the North Omaha community, specially the 68111 zip code of which the Triple One Neighborhood Association and Parents Union is the leading organizational/agency representative.

In compliance with the mandates of the Office of the Inspector General, TONAPU has issued several "independent and objective" reports, numerous letters and memos, and has continued to file injunctions against the city for its discriminatory abuse of Federal funds. Little has been done, which is why HUD is continually under attack for its lax monitoring of CDBG programs, not only in Omaha but around the nation.

We are requesting that the Office of the Inspector General conduct its investigations in conjunction with the North Omaha Development Advisory Board, headed by Cheryl Williams, to ensure objectivity and further, that these investigations of the City of Omaha Planning Department in the following areas: criminal, civil, and administrative. We will provide evidence, in writing and with testimony of residents, that will clearly establish all three.

The Office of the Inspector General offered up the following definition of what constitutes "fraud:" "Deliberate deception (by either false statement or omission) perpetrated for unlawful or unfair gain." This therefore makes fraud a crime committed against the low income minority residents of Nebraska in general, and North Omaha residents, in particular.

Matthew C. Stelly, Director
TONAPU

<u>Results of CDBG Abuse: Rise in Poverty and Violence</u>

PREFACE

This brief paper is a critical analysis of a news article written about violence in North Omaha. North Omaha is an area of the city that is predominantly black and it is the largest black community in the entire state. For that reason the article makes no mention of the racist conditions that gave rise to the segregated status of that community, and the long history of victimization that the area has undergone at the hands of city planners, developers, contractors, health care professionals, racist judges and attorneys and yes, police officers.

I have always believed that you should "never take away what you can't replace or improve." As a result, solutions to the violence are offered at the end of the essay. Existing leadership, black and white, is intellectually bankrupt when it comes to applying rockstrong solutions but instead, feed into the segregated conditions with their apathetic, nonchalant and Neanderthal actions and statements. The reporter who wrote the article that is about to be dissected, Henry Cordes, exacerbates the problem and, along with his fellow reporters at the major newspaper, serves to blame the residents of the ghetto for their condition, never pointing a finger at the group of officers that I have dubbed "buffoons in blue."

Following are my expert analyses of the situation. For those who disagree, debate the subject if you've got the guts. For those of you who agree, join in and help do something about these racists who occupy the status quo.

A 7-YEAR RETROSPECTIVE: VIOLENCE IN NORTH OMAHA

Today in June of 2017, it's more of the same. What this should tell even the most naïve of people is that crime in North Omaha is by design, that the cops aren't doing their jobs despite their on-going over-saturation in the black community, and that because of these two facts the city continues to qualify for more and more grant money from the government to "fight crime." It's a cyclical scam that has been taking place in and around Omaha and concentrated in the area's black and Latino communities, for more than five decades.

Seven years after the article that is about to be dissected appeared, the issue persists. This is therefore an analysis of an article by Henry J. Cordes of the Omaha World Herald titled, "Epidemic of Poverty, Violence." And of course, it is about the Omaha African-American community.

Cordes is usually an apologist for several Omaha institutions, with emphasis on the University of Nebraska Omaha. In this case, the February 21, 2010 article analyzed the symptoms of the problem but, as is the case with most of Cordes' articles, skips over the source or reasoning as to why the problem exists. My analyses will clear up this glaring *faux pas.*

The article starts off:

> Over a recent span of five days, gunfire rocked northeast Omaha.
> A teen gunned down outside a bowling alley.
> A 15-year-old shot in the face while walking to a bus stop.
> A man shot dead inside a home.(Cordes, 2010).

People like this reporter Cordes specialize in one thing: fluff pieces supporting white institutions and the usual stigma-laden reports from North

Omaha, although he doesn't have the guts to venture into the area. He's a coward for the most part, but this is par for the course when it comes to Omaha news reporters and the police: they arrive in time to take pictures of the bodies and to scrape up the bodies, respectively.

Another mission of the cowardly Cordes is to make it appear as if the deadpan strategies of the past actually work. For instance,

> **Stopping gun violence**
> VIGIL: A communitywide Stop the Violence rally and prayer service are set for tonight at 6 at Pilgrim Baptist Church, 2501 Hamilton St. (Cordes, 2010). OMAHA 360: To volunteer or assist in mentoring, gang intervention or other community initiatives aimed at eliminating gun violence, call the African-American Empowerment Network at 502-5153. (Cordes, 2010).

Rallies, prayer services and vigils haven't done a damn thing. These are the types of actions that cowardly black people take because they know what the problem is. The problem is that gangs control North Omaha because single parents kept telling those young punks that they were "the man of the house." These punks don't know what they're doing. As I proposed ten years ago, all you have to do is arrest the top 100 thugs in North Omaha and "crime" would disappear. But because the police use these guys for snitches, because the cops are involved in many ways, and because incoming grant money is dependent on crime continuing to take place, the situation remains the same.

As for Omaha 360, it is appropriately named. In a 360-degree turn, you end up in the same place where you started. And that is what these "negroes" – political leaders, the Empowerment Network, and those jive-ass ministers have been doing ever since they arrived (late) on the scene. But they receive praise and television coverage because they do nothing. And in doing nothing, the cops can keep applying for free Federal money coming from programs like Weed and Seed, Project Triggerlock, Project Safe Neighborhoods and other approaches that do nothing but provide money for more police overtime.

Continuing:

> A young woman shot in broad daylight, followed by a rolling gun battle through north Omaha streets. The surge of violence left three dead and another gravely wounded and heightened the tensions in several Omaha high schools. But more than that, it underscored how Omaha's streets in recent years have become among the deadliest places in America for blacks. (Cordes, 2010).

Instead of sucking the ass of the police reporters and the media that he works for, Cordes should be asking a key and essential question: "where are the cops when all this violence is taking place"? These young black kids have a field day because they have grown not to respect the police because they have learned that the police in Omaha are as dirty as any other "organized gang" that exists. The only difference is that when it comes to black people, it is clear that police have a veritable license to kill. Add that to the low regard that the cops have for North Omaha and the importance of violence reports to applying for future and on-going grant money from the government, and there are cop-based reasons for the violence that exists. But the Omaha World Herald and its top water-carrier continue to ignore these facts.

Instead, people like Cordes write the following:

> Fueled by gun violence in northeast Omaha, Nebraska has the
> third-highest black homicide rate in the nation, according to the
> latest compilation of detailed national homicide statistics.
> The figures are based on homicide data from 2007, but they aren't
> a one-year fluke. Nebraska's black homicide rate for 2008 was
> even worse, and should again rank with the nations highest when
> national figures become available. (Cordes, 2010).

See how these white people report it? Cordes is not alone: the local television stations do the same type of "the niggers are at it again" types of report orientations. The goal is to scare white Omahans into standing back and watching while cops get more money for doing much less while lying and claiming that they are "on the job." The white power structure and its media mouthpiece continue to claim that Nebraska's sky high rate is "fueled by gun violence in northeast Omaha." In other words, fueled by black people. What about those peckerwoods in the panhandle? What about the white people who bring the guns into the city? What about the gun violence waged by the cops themselves?

Nebraska doesn't give a damn about the "black homicide rate." It is that rate that justified the cops begging for more grant money from Federally-based programs like Weed and Seed, Project Safe Neighborhoods, Project Triggerlock, Community Oriented Policing and others. And most of that money goes for police overtime. And if that is the case and they are updating their cars, weaponry and technology, and they're getting more time on the streets, the only way that the "violence in northeast Omaha" could be going up is if those cops weren't doing their damn jobs or, even more likely, that they allow it to happen as they bide their time waiting for one of the most lucrative sweet deal pensions in the country.

Cordes (2010) provides much more information than he does relevant analysis of same. For instance:

> Nebraska's black homicide rate did drop considerably in 2009, a welcome change that police and north Omaha community leaders attribute to initiatives aimed at tamping down gun violence. But as the recent outburst of gunfire showed, there is still work to do."When we do have a flare-up like that, we absolutely pay attention," said Omaha Police Chief Alex Hayes. "All these efforts are still ongoing. It takes a collaborative effort."(Cordes, 2010).

The Omaha Police Division, like those so-called "community leaders" who are again speaking out after the fact, are collectively full of shit. The black homicide rate generates grant money for the cops, and major revenue for area hospitals who charge no less than seven thousand dollars to remove a bullet. Add to that the ambulance rides and the assignments created for a lily-white media, and hundreds of people benefit every time a black kid gets shot. No one wants to admit it because there are too many people attempting to make it look as if they are truly committed to ending the shootings. But in reality, nothing could be further from the truth.

The previous passage claims there are initiatives to "tamp down gun violence." Tamp it down? How about bringing it to an end the way cops do black lives? How about bringing it to a conclusion the way local employers do to black jobs and life chances? Tamping down gun violence means only to "lessen by degree" or "reduce." The definition is "to force in or down by repeated, rather light strokes." In other words, moderation. In other words incrementalism. In other words "take your time and do it in small steps." That is how the cops and those so-called community leaders approach black homicide because if they bring a sudden end to it, a major revenue stream – Weed and Seed, Project Triggerlock, Project Safe Neighborhoods – all come to an end. And when that happens that means no more police overtime.

Moving on:

> Both nationally and here, gangs, guns and black-on-black youth violence are at the center of the black homicide epidemic. Though Nebraska's 82,000 black residents make up about 4.5 percent of the state's 1.8 million population, blacks have accounted for nearly 40 percent of the state's homicide victims over the past three years. In Omaha, 55.5 percent of the homicide victims in that time were black. (Cordes, 2010).

Again, superficial analysis by Cordes, the fluff-piece writing racist. Let's explore the previous passage.

To begin with he writes that the guns and black on black violence "are at the center of the black homicide epidemic." If it is an epidemic then the "center" of it is moot; an epidemic is widespread and, in fact, the "middle" of one may be the safest place to be. It is the periphery, the outer edges, that have to be addressed and then a strategy to decrease the scope of the epidemic. If it was an epidemic white people would be more alarmed than they are; a pandemic includes a large area and a large proportion of a population. But in this case the deaths are locked into a certain sector of the city, one that is segregated and concentrated due to white folks and their redlining and blockbusting strategies.

Once we realize that black Omaha's area is concentrated to an eight square mile area of the city, then it is easier to see why black on black homicide takes place. There is a direct relationship between population density and conflict. Studies have been done on fruit flies in jars who turn on each other because they are locked in. The same applies to any creature that is forced into an area that is small and over populated. That is what the ghetto is. High population within limited space. Conflict is therefore inevitable

In other words, "conditions shape conduct and consciousness." White people have space and in some cases driveways that are wider than some public streets in North Omaha. There is a theory called "the frustration-aggression hypothesis" – the more frustrated a person or group gets, the greater is the tendency for aggression and conflict. North Omaha is dirt poor in a city that has one of the highest standards of living in the Midwest. Why is that? The kids know why and they rebel at the closest people to them. That is why segregation is so important; cowardly white people don't want black kids kicking them all off in their ass so they make sure that black people stay "holed up" and then those in power use an occupation force (police) to keep "those people" under control. Not "safe," but under control.

As a result,

> A black Nebraska resident during that span was 18 times more likely to be a victim of homicide than a white resident. That black-white disparity is much wider in Nebraska than the nation, where blacks are about seven times more likely to be a homicide victim. (Cordes, 2010).

This reporter, Henry Cordes, does all this research but he lives in a lily-white suburb. He is on the outside looking in. He knows all this but doesn't prompt his colleagues to write about the racism that is at the root of the statistics he just shared. They just stand by, watch it happen and then interview the cops sweep up the mess and then interview the teary-eyed relatives and friends of the victims. Then they wrap it all up and call it a "news report."

As a result of this newspaper nonchalance, this area media anomie and this mass malaise on the part of black witnesses and others who are affected, North Omaha remains in the crosshairs: no, not of the kids with the guns or gangs, but of an entire white-run system that has been "shooting down" the life chances of black people for decades. And therefore when you hear that local slogan that Omaha is "America's Best Kept Secret," you now know what the "secret" is: *we kill niggas.*
Want proof?

> That two of the recent victims were teenagers was hardly surprising. More than half of last year's black homicide victims were between 16 and 24, ages where many north Omaha youth are at high risk of falling into street gangs. Omaha police have identified 3,038 suspected gang members, up almost 300 from a year ago. (Cordes, 2010).

"Falling into street gangs," or being "lured" into them because of a system that has turned his back on them leaving them with few alternatives? There's a big difference, and Cordes knows it. This racist bastard has a responsibility to write articles where black people are made to look like their own worst enemies, where the ghetto is viewed as a "tangle of pathology" or a "culture of disadvantage" and rarely as an intentionally designed and maintained enclave that serves a purpose that is similar to that of a maximum security prison.

White people fear any manifestation of black unity and indeed, have waged subtle and overt wars against such. Remember the FBI and the attacks on the Black Panther Party? Remember the attacks on the Symbionese Liberation Army, killing them while believing the easily assembled lies of the white girl Patty Hearst? Remember the assassination of Dr. Martin Luther King, Jr., which they blamed on someone else? Remember the assassination of Malcolm X, which they blamed on someone else? And the list goes on and on. Black youth gangs are unified if nothing else and the white man uses his own gang – the gang in blue – to harass, arrest and when possible, murder these black kids off by pitting them against one another.

The white folks in charge did not get where they got by permitting their enemies a lot of leisure time. Take note of the following fact:

> Guns were the weapon used in nearly nine of 10 slayings of black residents in Nebraska over the past three years — including all 15 in 2009. And in the vast majority of cases where the shooter was identified, the shooter also was black. (Cordes, 2010).

So it's not just the young people – its people from various age groups. And what is the common denominator? It's location, location, location. And the white cops are bent on making sure that the killings remain confined to a given area of the city. And that area is North Omaha – the black community. And the fact that this kind of activity is taking place in black enclaves all over America makes it clear that there is another "plan by design": and that plan is to stir up problems in an area that is already dense in population, fan the flames of gang warfare, set up a snitch system and the leak out information on who the snitches are, and then stand back and watch the bodies fall one-by-one.

As a result,

> "It tends to be intra-racial, focused in urban centers, and guns are the weapon of choice," said Josh Sugarmann of the Washington-based Violence Policy Center. The toll goes beyond the victims and the people who loved them. There were children in north Omaha during the recent eruption of violence who saw people they knew gunned down in front of them. (Cordes, 2010).

Cordes contacts some Jew in Washington DC so that he can get told what any local scholar could have told him. It's "intra-racial" because segregation keeps all black people in the same area to make sure that the violence doesn't become "inter-racial." The way Cordes frames the article it seems that black people kill each other for comic relief. He writes nothing of Omaha's racial segregation, its high black unemployment rate (especially among young black males), and the long-time racist maltreatment of black people in the areas of jurisprudence, health care, and education. It's the frustration-aggression hypothesis all over again.

The "negroes" who have been anointed "black leaders" are the worst crop of community people that North Omaha has ever seen. They are truly coons of a most embarrassing stripe. For instance,

> Willie Barney of the African-American Empowerment Network, a community action group in north Omaha, said the Nebraska statistics and recent violence are sobering. But he said he's been encouraged by the community reaction in the days following the latest shootings. Not only in north Omaha but in neighborhoods far beyond, people are saying loud and clear: It's time to stop the killing. (Cordes, 2010).

To begin with, the African American Empowerment Network is no "community action group" because there is no action associated with them. They are a group named by Susie Buffett and also controlled by same. They are people who know nothing about community work and all they have is a slick magazine which is ironically called "Revive!" and every month or so they have a "by invitation only" community meeting where they feed black people and while the people eat, these Empowerment negroes pontificate a slate of general truisms that have not been applied and cannot be applied. In simple terms, this group constitutes a "buffer zone" between the white man and the black poor.

Secondly, how could this negro Willie Barney be "encouraged" by "reactions" to shootings? Those responses haven't prompted any solutions or haven't serve to quell future shootings. This is vintage Barney-like thinking: ass backwards and incomplete. Now comes the coup de grace.

The previous paragraph concludes, "Not only in north Omaha but in neighborhoods far beyond, people are saying loud and clear: It's time to stop the killing." Says who? Those who are "far beyond" the ghetto – how far are they? And if they are "far beyond," then of what business is it what takes place in the black community when those hinterland residents live out there because of their disdain for black people? Cordes, the reporter, is one of those people and it's reflected in his jejune choices of people to interview as well as his interpretations of black social reality.

Now, more "rubble" from Barney (get it?):

> But to make a difference, he said, such words need to be turned
> into action by expanding street intervention programs that reach
> out to gang members, providing more mentors and viable activities
> as alternatives to gangs, and implementing new training and
> employment programs. All will require money, manpower and
> focus. (Cordes, 2010).

Stop white people from invading the black community, fight against white racism, and keep sick negroes like Barney at a distance. Once these ideas that I offer are implemented, then we will be able to better ascertain who the assholes are who are leading the gangs. As I proposed ten years ago, on the air during an interview on KKAR's "Talk of the Town," if you arrest the top 100 thugs in North Omaha there will be NO crime. But these peckerwoods know that if they truly attacked the problem, there goes the grant money. And this brings us to Barney's asinine ideas.

All of what he proposed are also job creating grant "programs" for white people. It's called "the social service approach." He calls for "expanding street intervention" which means more police-based programs and projects; he calls for providing mentors – additional programs for missionary-minded white people; he calls for training and employment programs. All these are based on begging the government for money to employ white people and desperate negroes. And it's been done since the 1960s. And since the programs are not outcome based, since there is no end game, the programs continue to fail – as they were designed to do.

"When you say 'Enough is enough,' the next step is, what are you going to do about it?" Barney said. "This is a critical juncture for Omaha." Though concern about gun violence in Omaha's black community is not new, what wasn't known until now was how the violence has made Nebraska among the deadliest places for blacks (Cordes, 2010).

Remember, this was written seven years ago. So what does Barney know about a "critical juncture"? He still has his bullshit job carrying water for Susie Buffett and other white people. His so-called "empowerment network" hasn't empowered a single soul other than white people who are coming into North Omaha in droves to develop, dig, construct, renovation, tear down, destroy, and benefit from the takeover. The negative demographics get worse and the white man gets richer from the incursion into North Omaha. And Willie Barney and the rest of those Uncle Toms have been and continue to be part and parcel of the "white takeover."

As the previous paragraph makes clear, the violence is getting worse. And once reason for it is because of the "buffoons in blue" (the title of another manuscript I've produced on the subject of the Omaha Police Division). These cops couldn't find a hooker in a whore house. They're fat, out of shape, and ride around the community burning up taxpayers' gas and arrive on the scene only AFTER a crime is committed or someone's been shot. These janitors in Kevlar vests are overpaid and have one of the best pension plans in the nation. Why work hard? The more crime, the more police overtime. The more overtime, the bigger the flat screen TV in the man-cave at their suburban homes.

Now, evidence of police buffoonery appears below:

That's largely because Omaha homicide statistics haven't been reported into a detailed FBI national homicide database for almost two decades. A Violence Policy Center study based on that FBI database and released last month found that Nebraska ranked 42nd in black homicide rate. But the study included only the five black homicides in 2007 that occurred outside of Omaha. (Cordes, 2010).

No report of homicide statistics into a detailed FBI national homicide data base – as required – for twenty years! So what were these assholes doing all that time? They were at their desks, they saw the computers, they had the data and they knew the roles. And they just ignored it. Nebraska may ranks 42nd in black homicides because there are no blacks anywhere outside of Omaha! The plan and intent is to confine and destroy black communities, and there is only one: North Omaha! A conspiracy can easily be established – so why doesn't milquetoast reporter Henry Cordes write about THAT?

Continuing:

> When the 22 black homicide victims from Omaha are added to the
> study, Nebraska shoots up to third in per-capita black homicide
> rate, behind Pennsylvania and Missouri. Nebraska's rate of 34
> homicides per 100,000 black population in 2007 was 65 percent
> above the national rate. (Cordes, 2010).

As I said, the examination should be of the culture that produced the gun, the murderer and the victim. That would be the city of Omaha. David Bristow wrote a book called A Dirty, Wicked Town: Tales of 19th Century Omaha. If you changed the number "19th Century" to "21st Century," the title would still fit like a glove.

Cordes' belated commentary continues:

> If the Omaha numbers are added to the group's two previous
> studies, Nebraska ranked 14th in 2006 and eighth in 2005, its per-
> capita rate in both years well above the national average.
> But violence surged even higher in 2007 and 2008, pushing
> Nebraska's rate among the very highest. Even with the significant
> drop in homicides in 2009 — from 28 down to 15 — Nebraska's
> rate fell to only slightly below the typical national average.
> (Cordes, 2010).

There is an analogy I'd like to use as it relates to Cordes' previous asinine discussion of a "drop" in homicides from 28 to 15.

A man is walking down the street. The police pull over, grab and cuff him and throw him in the car. Once at the station with no explanation, he is booked and then thrown into a holding cell. Later, he appears before a judge and is given a long sentence, still with no explanation. Once in prison he is placed in solitary confinement for weeks. At the end of the period in solitary, he is allowed to go out into "the big yard" with the rest of the inmates. To some people – people like Henry Cordes – this man has made "progress" because he is no longer in solitary. But to those of us with an active brain stem, we know it's not progress because he should have never been arrested in the first place.

But that's what white people do. They dig a ditch and put black people into it and then call it progress when black people crawl out of a ditch that they should not have ever been placed into in the first place. As Malcolm X once asked. "Why should we be grateful to a man who takes a knife *halfway* out of our backs?" So Nebraska's black homicide rate may have "fallen," but the reason why it was high in the first place was because of the conditions created by racist and segregationist-thinking white folks.

Moving on:

> Police Chief Hayes and north Omaha leaders said that the high
> rankings may be startling at first but shouldn't surprise anyone in
> light of the similarly high poverty rates and dropout rates seen
> among Omaha blacks in recent years. (Cordes, 2010).

Again we have the reference to the "North Omaha leaders." What are they leading? Who do they lead? What plans or paradigms have they developed? The plans I offered them on television and in writing are rejected because these plans involve something that these "negroes" are not willing to do: confront the white man, who is the source of our problems! Without that, there is nothing that can be done. In other terms, Christian soldiers, "without practice, preaching is of little use"!

The high poverty rates persist and the dropout rates remain because black people are not prepared and refuse preparation. Instead, they listen to white people who come into town and give grandiose speeches, follow blindly behind ass-backwards school superintendents and chancellors, and then quietly collect paychecks. The kids suffer while the "negroes" pay their mortgages on houses outside of the black community and car notes that enable them to drive to those houses! This is the way it has been at least since 1977 when I first arrived in the River City!

The white reporter who knows next to nothing about black culture or the black community that is less than three miles from the newspaper that he works at, sure knows how to consult the documents, studies and even the census so that he can "learn more about the nig … oops! I mean "negro" people. For instance,

> The latest U.S. Census survey indicates Omaha has the 11th-
> highest black poverty rate among the nation's 100 largest metro
> areas. At least three national studies in recent years have found
> Nebraska to have among the highest dropout rates for blacks, each
> putting the rate at more than 50 percent. (Cordes, 2010).

So the dropout rate is high and so is the poverty rate. Henry Cordes has been in Omaha all that time as have his bosses and co-workers at the Omaha World Herald. And even with a lone black reporter, Sibyl Myers (who has been deceased for a decade), they never "assigned" anyone to talk to the black residents and ask them their feelings about racism, segregation and the white man's discriminatory tendencies. It's always the "examine the victim" approach or "write a story about the outcomes of what whites have done without mentioning whites as the perpetrators." And as a result of this systemic approach to "reporting," Omaha's abuse of black people and the conditions they live under persists, with Cordes and the newspaper acting as co-conspirators.

Black responses to what takes place are carefully selected, making sure that those who are asked to respond are clueless and without any sense of history or black culture. Witness the following case in point:

> "I'm extremely disturbed by those numbers, but I'm not surprised
> by those numbers," said Ben Gray, the Omaha city councilman
> who represents north Omaha. "It goes hand in hand with the
> poverty we see and the racial separation which is obvious to
> anyone who comes to this town."(Cordes, 2010).

Ben has not done a damn thing to address the poverty that he claims to have seen. Although he takes credit for bringing a Wal-Mart to the black community (which is a Donald Trump-sized lie), he has done nothing but TALK. He has accepted money under the table to bring a CVS Pharmacy to an area of town that is not even in his district. He is a notorious liar and maker of promises that he never keeps. Violence persists under his watch and some would argue that it has gotten worse since he's become the City Council representative. He is now on his third term meaning that the Christians and "negro leaders" who vote for him also need their asses collectively kicked.

More foolish selection of people who are supposed to be "in the know" continues and the result – an article that contains words but doesn't say shit – continues on, unabated:

> When the director of the State Office of Violence Prevention sees
> the numbers, he sees the reason his office was created in 2009. It's
> likely no coincidence, Mike Friend said, that lawmakers were
> moved to act in the wake of violence we now know was among the
> nation's most severe. (Cordes, 2010).

The office was created in 2009 – as if homicides in the black community had just started. Omaha was conceived in violence. Had Cordes given a shit and done some research, he would come across articles like the one by C.V. McKanna, Jr., titled, "). Seeds of destruction: Homicide, race and justice in Omaha, 1880-1920, " an office engaged in some form of "violence prevention" should have been started a hundred years ago.

Let me remind you of why that should have been the case before we move on: Operating from the thesis that homicides by blacks on blacks and against whites was something that came with blacks who came from the south – as a matter of personal pride – McKanna (1994) documents some interesting facts which will be shared below:

> H.J. Walker, the victim mentioned in the Omaha World Herald
> headline, had arrived in Omaha from Ouray, Colorado, a few hours
> previous to the shooting and had been drinking heavily all day.
> After entering Garrity's Saloon on Friday evening, Walker took a
> table and told stories about ranch life on the high plains. He was
> soon surrounded by "women with painted cheeks and scarlet
> dresses and rough men who laughed long and loudly at the coarse
> jests and uncouth stories he told." (p. 65).

The conditions of this hick town having been established, now let us interject the variable of racism:

> When Pat Jackson, an African-American entertainer hired to
> provide music, contributed a personal story about horses and cattle,
> the boisterous rancher made some racial remarks. A witness stated:
> "The cow puncher didn't like having him butt in that way and
> called the coon names." Walker threatened to teach Jackson some
> manners. According to a witness, "Jackson wouldn't stand for that
> kind of talk and says, "I guess you won't." and with that he pulls
> out a gun and plugged the puncher." Jackson fired two shots in
> quick succession from a Smith and Wesson .38 revolver. Walker
> slumped to the floor, mortally wounded (McKanna, 1994).

And there you have it. According to McKanna,

> This shooting in Garrity's Saloon at Tenth Street and Capitol
> Avenue, in the middle of the brothel district typified violent
> behavior in Omaha at the beginning of the twentieth century. Since
> men visited saloons armed with concealed weapons, particularly
> handguns, it is not surprising that violent confrontations often
> ended in death. However, this homicide s particularly significant
> because of the interracial factor – black kills white (McKanna,
> 1994: 66).

Like the racist Henry Cordes in 2010, McKanna contended that there was a "subculture of violence" that existed in the black community of Omaha between 1880 and 1920. And further, McKanna attributed that violence to black people from the South, having been abused badly there, coming to Omaha and bent on not taking any of the white man's shit, including insults to their manhood. More specifically, McKanna surmises:

> A majority of the blacks in Omaha migrated from the South, with
> 79 and 77 percent for the 1900 and 1910 Census, respectively.
> They came to Omaha not only looking for economic opportunity,

> but also to escape an oppressive system of tyranny enforced by
> white lynch law. They brought with them a heritage of violence –
> in essence, a "subculture of violence." Two sociologists found that
> African Americans born in the South and who moved to the North
> had higher homicide rates than blacks born and raised in the North
> … Young black men involved in homicide witnessed violence or
> know relatives who experienced violence at the hands of southern
> whites (McKanna, 1994: 67)

See? You see white folks (today it's the cops) shooting down black people with impunity and you do the same thing. You turn on the video games, the television set or go to the movies and peckerwoods are getting away with murder like there's no tomorrow. So in order to defend yourself and your so-called "dignity" (today the young people are going around talking about being "disrespected"), you lash out with a gun. But back in the day the behavior went far beyond "self-defense," but also had a lot to do with one's pride and honor, as McKanna explains:

> They carried with them their cultural tradition that included a
> propensity to settle problems, especially those that concerned
> "honor," with force, that often could be lethal … Honor became a
> cult iin the South that had to be defended at all costs … Slavery
> and the plantation reinforced the tendency toward violence …
> African Americans accepted this "code of honor" within their
> culture (McKanna, 1994: 68).

What is today's American if not "wage slavery"? And if white folks are having it imposed on them and have accepted it as a way of life, just IMAGINE how black people feel. We see inferior whites, unqualified crackers and pitiful peckerwoods making money and getting jobs that a black person could do much better. I know two black PhDs who are driving the city bus.

The same way white women claimed to feel about their women and the myth of sacred white womanhood is the way that black men TRULY felt about black women, who we recognized as being the key to the race. McKanna explains:

> … The foundation of southernness lies in the attitudes of whites
> who dominated blacks. White southerners developed their own
> unwritten "ten commandments"." The first four dealt with the
> "protection of women against "rape, adultery, seduction, or
> "slander against chastity.'" Physical violence by a male relative of
> the offended woman was the only acceptable response for any of
> these offenses. Any lie or "opprobrious epithets" were considered
> insults and each one was "equal to a blow" or any other form of
> assault. It was common to use physical force, often lethal, to settle

> any of these forms of grievances. … southerners are more likely to
> be violent when "honor" is at stake, particularly in love triangles or
> family disputes (McKanna, 1994: 67-68).

When black Southerners came to Omaha, our people came here to work. We didn't come here to start any shit with the white man. But if he dared to talk shit or start that name-calling stuff, we were more than happy to kick his ass with our fists or, if necessary, to bust a cap. This tradition still exists by both races: witness the white boys who thought they were just going to "teach these niggers a lesson" as our kids got off the buses during forced integration. Many of those white kids went home with three pair s of shoes: the two on their feet and one sticking out of the crack of their asses!

And,

> Many [Blacks] had a great disdain for white imposed law.
> African-Americans from the South viewed southern courts as
> "instruments of injustice and oppression and upon those convicted
> in them as martyrs and victims" … Frustrated by being trapped
> within a ghetto controlled by an unjust system and carrying with
> them a "code of honor," Omaha's African Americans often reacted
> by resorting to violence, sometimes with the slightest provocation
> (McKanna, 1994: 69).

McKanna makes a major mistake in the first statement of the previous paragraph. He writes that, "Many [Blacks] … had a great disdain for white imposed law." Wrong. Black people had a disdain for the mis-application of the law or laws that were designed to deprive black people of their rights. We knew, first of all, that the laws were made by lawless men. But even in that we never resisted them unless these laws somehow infringed on our rights. That is when the ass whipping's were dished out.

And how is that different from today? These kids aren't going to be pushed around and called "nigger" over a cops loudspeaker. These kids aren't going to be manhandled by some frustrated peckerwood grade school teacher. Times have changed and white people are growing fearful that black people see through their racist bullshit. So when McKanna writes, "Omaha's African-Americans often reacted by resorting to violence, sometimes with the slightest provocation." Again, like the writers of today, seeking to blame the victim. What is a "slight provocation" to a white man when it is being imposed on blacks might be an anvil across the head!

The nail in the coffin of McKanna's racist and yet relevant essay can be found in the following truth-claims:

> The number of actual homicides did not increase dramatically
> until the period 1902-1910. A decade or more confined to low-
> paying, demeaning work, segregated housing, racist behavior by
> saloon keepers and other white merchants, and racial mistrust
> created tremendous pressure on Omaha's black population. In
> conjunction with southernness exhibited by blacks, these factors
> may have caused an increase in the socialization of aggression,
> with African-American hostility then turning outward against both
> black and white victims (McKanna, 1994: 71-72).

What McKanna describes and then seeks to attribute solely to black people who have been "socialized" to be aggressive is again, a case of calling the white kettle a peckerwood. How did black people learn this aggression against another race? From the original racist killer himself: whitey. He did it to the Native American, to the Chinese immigrant, to Mexicans during the war and of course, through enslavement of black people. All black people have seen from these American "Christians" has been the heel of their boots. And white bitches stood by and watched and applauded. What did they EXPECT the result to be? Perhaps black people asking, "Might I have another?"

Furthermore, there can never be real "equality" when white racism can call upon mob law when it pleases. Bitzes (1970) documents an incident in 1891 shows the unique racial character of Omaha, as blacks joined a white lynch mob of some 500 persons to help kill George Smith, a black man accused of assaulting a five-year-old girl. Today, it is accepted that Smith was innocent (p. 201). And to this day, there are a number of blacks who have "joined" the system to oppress the majority of those who reside in the near North Side. More on this later in the book.

McKanna (1994) subjectively describes the early living arrangements for blacks upon arriving in Omaha and settling in:

> … the redlight district that blossomed around a core of saloons
> and brothels, concentrated between Douglas and Davenport from
> Eighth to Fourteenth Streets. This region became Omaha's
> "tenderloin" district, an area heavily involved in vice, crime, and
> alcohol … The large number of saloons within the redlight district
> (fifty-eight in and an additional sixty-four within a three-block
> radius) acted as the only place where African Americans and
> whites mixed on a social level and, in some cases, bar owners
> practiced discrimination. Saloons became "hot points" for racial
> interaction that could become violent (McKanna, 1994).

The situation in and around Omaha's black community is not much different today. Although there are fewer bars, comparatively speaking, lounges and taverns remain a staple in the area. And more importantly, the same peckerwood who was supposed to be in charge of "law and order" back then is still calling the shots today; hence, the same violence-oriented tendencies.

Now we can put Cordes' ass-backwards writings into proper perspective as he opines,

> Indeed, the escalating gun violence in 2007 and 2008 — including a month in the summer of 2007 when there were 31 shootings citywide in 31 days — got a lot of people's attention. Police responded by cracking down on illegal gun possession and collaborating more in the community, seeking to break a culture that discouraged "snitching" in the shootings' wake. (Cordes, 2010).

Police can't "crack down on illegal gun possession." In Omaha a "crackdown" means that they may have confiscated one or two. These hicks wouldn't know how to conduct a crackdown if they tripped on one. If they could "crack down" so much, then why the near pandemic? Why the escalation of gun violence? That shows that the "crackdown" is just a dream – and what is a dream? A dream is "hope without a plan." And that's what white people sell to black people through that Dr. Martin Luther King, Jr., bullshit and the on-going lectures from preachers, ministers and near-illiterate "negro" community leaders.

Want proof? Take note:

> Gray, Barney and other north Omaha leaders launched the Impact One intervention program to open lines of communication with gangs and stop retaliatory killings. Some of the program's counselors are former gang members, giving them credibility in efforts to lure youths to more productive lives. (Cordes, 2010).

That was in 2010. Here we are seven years later and you haven't heard a single word about so-called "Impact One," have you? You can't open up lines with gang bruthas when you fear them, when you deride them and blame them for the problem the way that Ben Gray, Willie Barney and other "negroes" tend to do. And that "former gang member as counselor" scam has been run for so long that people are actually beginning to think it works. The only people who benefit are the "former gang members" who get a pay check for making promises and promoting more "dreams" – hope without a plan.

What is offered are pacification programs and appeasement-oriented projects aimed at kicking the can down the road. For instance:

> A summer jobs program for at-risk youths started modestly in 2008
> and then, through federal stimulus funds, expanded to 500 kids in
> 2009, giving them work experience, some income and keeping
> them off the streets. The entire anti-violence campaign has grown
> into Omaha 360, a coalition of business, philanthropic, community
> and faith groups inside and outside north Omaha. (Cordes, 2010).

The summer jobs program started in 1964 with the Economic Opportunity Act, and varying versions of it have been on-going because of white people's fears of black people setting cities on fire. What Omaha's Johnny-come-lately responses do is to copy that which has already been underway elsewhere. The summer jobs in Omaha are just a way for the city to further abuse Community Development Block Grant monies – money that is supposed to be ENTIRELY spent on North Omaha, not just a few pieces of chump change that these peckerwoods dole out to keep black kids from fucking them up.

Next quote comes from a former police chief, a true coon who is now the director of the Urban League of Nebraska – another "do nothing" nonprofit that sits around begging for grant money. Check out what this negro has to say:

> A key test for the effort, said Urban League of Nebraska Chief
> Executive Thomas Warren, will be finding funds for an expanded
> youth job and training program this summer. There were
> noticeable drops in violence during months the program was in
> place, the former Omaha police chief said. Mayor Jim Suttle has
> been lobbying for more federal dollars, and other sources are being
> explored. (Cordes, 2010).

The white man knew what he was doing; no sooner did Warren "retire" as the head cop he literally "slid" right into the directorship of the Urban League. And that organization has been stifled, stymied and stagnant ever since. And being the coon that he is, he mouths general truisms combined with a tidbit of bullshit, as the following quote clearly bears out:

> "Even as chief, I always felt violent crime was a symptom of
> poverty," Warren said. "If we're going to prevent violent crime, we
> have to start dealing with the causes, including under-education
> and lack of employment." Barney said everyone in the community
> has a role to play. "Not everyone is a gang intervention specialist,"
> he said, "but you can be a mentor."(Cordes, 2010).

Barney forgets one thing: *the blind cannot lead the blind*. The backward negro cannot produce anything but another backwards negro, and that is what's wrong with these mentoring programs today. They're either made up of white bitches trying to coddle young black girls and be their buddies, or white boys trying to take black males out to shoot hoop where they (the white boys) can get dunked on. Or if not that, then it's a mentoring program whose goal it is to funnel black kids into some kind of bullshit "boy scout" like way of thinking. And when that is the goal, then they bring in black males, dress them in goony outfits, and force the kids to do the same.

Cordes' article is lacking in the same was as the media in Omaha is lacking: in cultural competency, insight and historical knowledge. "Violence in North Omaha" is the product of violence that has been waged against black people by white Omahans for at least two centuries.

And it appears that things haven't changed much

TOWARD ROCKSTRONG SOLUTIONS

The month following the discovery of police malfeasance and the attempted cover up by the Omaha World Herald (March of 2010), I started what would be a 5-part series on "Violence in Omaha," which was published in the *Omaha Star* newspaper. Following are all five of those installments and, as you can see, I included a plethora of proposals for public consideration.

<u>Preliminary Notes</u>
Violence in Nebraska and the Northside: Beyond Mythology
To Meaningful Solutions (Part I of a 5-part series)

Before we can arrive at some sensible solutions to dealing with violence we have to first of all make sure that we are asking the correct questions and that those reporting it are telling the truth. Flawed inquiry has, throughout Omaha history, led to solutions that really only served to make the problem worse. And one way that those problems get worse is when people who don't know feel an obligation to act as if they do. Surrounded by microphones and story-starved rookie reporters, these social novices mimic what they've heard others say or utter theories that are more fiction than fact.

Now is the time for conceptual clarity, not confusion. Hence, the following 5-part series on violence, courtesy of the Uhuru Sasa Research Institute. Let us begin with some preliminary notes.

According to a recent day-late, dollar-short "report," "Omaha's streets have become among the deadliest places in America for blacks." But the report is flawed when it says that this has been the case "in recent years." They could not have been more wrong.

If by "recent years" you mean for the past century, then you are correct. But violence is not an issue until it impacts upon suburban life or the city's budget. Only when it comes to THEIR well-being does the "oh-my-gosh-what's happening" reaction come to the fore. In this case, let's begin with a little history.

There is a publication called the Journal of American Ethnic History. In the Fall, 1994 edition there was an article by Clare McKanna titled, "Seeds of Destruction: Homicide, Race and Justice in Omaha, 1880-1920." This article shows that the concept of "recent" is relative, and that issues of race and homicide are as native to Omaha as the Mormon Bridge.

Read the article and you find that back in the day, which was in the area between Douglas and Davenport, and from 8th to 14th Streets, was an area that was known as "the tenderloin district." It was an area where you could find all the dope, alcohol, pimps and prostitutes you wanted. You could find a dice game, a gambling house (if not there, then nearby) and it was an area where there were a number of bars, then known as "saloons."

Now, check this out: in this small area of but a few square miles, there were 58 saloons, and another 64 when you came over to what is now the northside (because of segregation, of course). In the latter set of places, blacks and white would drink together, despite the discrimination and there was a great deal of violence.

Now, fast forward to 2010: North Omaha still has more bars per square mile than any other sector of the city (with south Omaha probably a close second), and although the gambling shacks are gone, they have been replaced with dope houses – all places that cops know exist. Alcohol, drugs and today's version of vice: pit bull dog fights. Contextual similarities create similarity in conduct, people! Violence a hundred years ago and violence today in the 21st century. Recent? Don't make me laugh.

The only thing that may be different is that there is LESS integration involved in the area. This is why there is less attention being paid to the area unless somehow, white folks are affected. If they weren't affected black homicide would not be considered a "problem;" it would be viewed as "business as usual."

One source reports the issue with half-truth, half-fantasy as it offers the following: *Fueled by gun violence in northeast Omaha, Nebraska has the third-highest black homicide rate in the nation, according to the latest compilation of detailed national homicide statistics. The figures are based on homicide data from 2007, but they aren't a one-year fluke. Nebraska's black homicide rate for 2008 was even worse, and should again rank with the nation's highest when national figures become available. Nebraska's black homicide rate did drop considerably in*

2009, a welcome change that police and north Omaha community leaders attribute to initiatives aimed at tamping down gun violence.

To begin with, how can a statewide set of stats be fueled by an area of 8 square miles on the northeastern sector of Omaha? What provides the fuel? Who fuels the fire? Neglect. No, not by the police: their job, by their own admission, is to simply sweep up the mess after its been made. I have them on record making that claim. No, it is the neglect of these "community leaders" who don't have a clue but "on the island of the blind, the one-eyed man is king." Feel me?

People who are considered leaders in North Omaha couldn't cut it anywhere else (except for Sen. Chambers). That's why they're here. And their presence here is not to solve problems because were it not for problems, there would be no need for outsiders to approach them for ANYTHING. These leaders get asked "the negro questions" and are approached to find out "what's wrong with your people?" Other than that, there is nothing for these "leaders" to do because, as you can see, they ain't leadin'!!!

So there was neglect then that was patronized by the existence of a "Black mayor" who represented black people's viewpoints. And today, there may be more token representation, but ask yourself this question: if the problem has existed over 100 years, and we've been here all this time, how can we just say it's the cops? One brother said that he links the problem to poverty, but if that is the case, what happened to the more than $200 million that this city has gotten since 1975 in Community Development Block Grant funds? So it's not just the lack of black leadership, it's the greediness of white leadership. This reality places the issue in the laps of human beings, and not on some abstract concept like "poverty," which is also a human invention (i.e., how did it come about? Why isn't there poverty all over Omaha? Why are some people rich while North Omahans are poor? Etc.)

Let us continue this progression in logic – something that, thus far, has been non-existent in the discussion of the topic.

Statements like "recent outbursts show there is still work to do" and "flare-ups" shroud the problem in the collective ignorance of decision makers. I have clearly shown that violence in Omaha has an historical character, and that includes North Omaha.

Nebraska ranks number three for a reason. Although there are few blacks, the ones that are here have been fodder for the creation of thousands of jobs for white folks. From social workers, intake workers, case workers, and heads of various "commissions," black poverty translates to mean big bucks for Nebraska in general, and Omaha in particular. Let me, once again, show you how it's done.

In order to quality for most of these grants (from Weed and Seed, Project Triggerlock, Community Oriented Policing grants, Project Safe Neighborhoods, Community Development Block Grant, Community Service Block Grant, etc.), your city has to have population that is sizable enough to have what the government calls "a pocket of poverty." In Omaha, that means YOU.

What the people who work for the City and County do is document all the negative things that they will FIX and MEND if they are given the money. They document high unemployment, low median housing value, high crime rate, high teen pregnancy rate, low median income and so on. They put this info on a proposal and send it in. Then they get a big, fat check from the Feds. And then, guess what happens: they FORGET about the population whose poverty qualified them for the money in the first place.

This, in my view, is as much a form of violence as a judo cop across the neck or a kick to the groin. All these acts are acts of aggression and create great pain. In the case of grant abuse, however, the pain is cumulative and long-term. Look around you and ask: with all these grant programs, why does North Omaha continue to stay poor? The answer is simple: because with no "pocket of poverty" Omaha – an otherwise all-American city – wouldn't qualify for federal money!

Welfare! That's what it is. These people know that their citizens are not the smartest in the world. That's why it's hard to get corporations to relocate here despite the ambience, access to the river and so on. So they have to write grants and keep beggin' for money so they can pay their bills and hire their own people. Sure, some of us get jobs out of it; but since we make up a disproportionate number of the poor, we should get more than we've been getting.

Then look at how they say that the violence makes Nebraska one of the deadliest places for blacks. Here's my question: if the violence is so profound, wouldn't that make it a violent place for anyone? That is, unless, those doing the reporting are ADMITTING that Nebraska is so segregated that the only place a black person will meet with a threat is if he goes to the one area of the state where blacks actually live – North Omaha!

So their own words and reports indict them in their role in creating a set of conditions that are conducive to anti-social conduct – in this case, black-on-black homicide.

In the days ahead you will hear about request for "More federal dollars," "more grant money," and "hiring more cops." You will hear people talking about the need for "more mentors, more role models" or "more church attendance."

These might be solutions that Omaha is smugly satisfied with offering, but they've been offered before because the same people who watched the problem snowball remain in power. Then they hand the racist neglect down to their progeny.

Now, with these preliminary notes out of the way, the next four installments will offer up critical analysis and REAL and ROCKSTRONG solutions. So take notes – help is on the way!

Part 2:
Violence in Nebraska and the Northside: Maintaining the Money-Machine Through Mayhem, Misconduct and 'Cultural Miasma"

Again, this five-part series is a response the correction to the "report" that the state of Nebraska ranks third in the nation when it comes to black-on-black homicides. Last week I pointed out the tip of the iceberg regarding the grants-related "scams" that are run in order to generate federal dollars for Omaha to fight problems in the Northside, fights that they intentionally forget to arrive at once the grant checks arrive.

<u>Mayhem</u>

Homicide is defined as the killing of one human being by another. And most of you view this in a physical sense. But those of us who think for ourselves understand that a person can "die" in a number of ways that go beyond the ceasing of biological functions. When John Rambo (Sylvester Stallone) tore up an entire town in the movie, "First Blood," his response as to why he did was a simple, "He drew first blood," in reference to a brutal sheriff (Brian Dennehey) who had harassed him constantly.

The same can be said here in Nebraska. If the claims of the state being third in black-on-black homicide are correct (and later I'll argue that they are not), then this is nothing more than "payback" to a system that "drew first blood." So the mayhem I'm talking about is not in regard to the shootings, shenanigans and shut-in elders of North Omaha: I'm talking about the Mayhem created by the people that created the conditions where these killings are a matter-of-fact.

Mayhem, as you may know, is defined as, "needless or willful violence or damage." Those in power are so busy pointing their fingers at the state's only real black community that they forget one thing: those responsible for maintaining the conditions that foster and foment violence should be the ones who are identified as the source of the problem.

In a 7-part series that I wrote last year about the Department of Labor (after which time the director "coincidentally resigned"), I showed how that division plays a role in maintaining on-going endemic black poverty. The mayhem is willful and needless, as those who need help the most don't get it; the only "assistance" that is received (they call it "assistance" because to "help" is positive, but assistance can mean anything) is assisting black folks to remain dependent upon the system. In order to get this, you have to attend this workshop or meeting which, of course, is being supervised by someone who has a job because of YOUR poverty. You get this stipend, but can only spend it with someone or some business that is not in North Omaha; you get "awarded" this scholarship, which you never see, but those who sell the books and charge the tuitions get to see the real CASH.

These are but a few of the forms of "assistance" that black folks in Nebraska have received over the decades. They fix your house only because they wrote a grant and got money to do so; they offer you medical assistance only if you have insurance that they can abuse; they want to "make you safe" by assigning the youngest, most inexperienced (and oftentimes most racist) police officers to your 'hood. Willful – and needless.

This is how violence is set and then fanned. Closing down black day care centers in a certain zip code that just so happens to be in the core of North Omaha, while creating newer and bigger centers that are run by white folks who, by the way, give a preference to Title XX families (subsidized by the state). Can you say,"mo' money, mo' money, mo' money??"

This is but a small chunk of the state's responsibility for the violence that they claim emanates from North O. All these departments, headed by people who know little or nothing about cultural competency, using guesswork and flawed data, drew "first blood" against a people that at one time were humble to a fault. In 1975 WOWT concluded, following a community survey, that "Omaha is host to one of the most law-abiding ghettos in the country."

Add that to a state that is overwhelmingly white and rural, and for these people to point out North Omaha as the reason for their rise in violence against blacks is not only hypocritical, but contemptible.

Misconduct

This incredibly insightful response to the "report" about all this violence is based on a media-fanned assumption that the information is correct. I merely use the opportunity to raise the consciousness of people of color and point out, to those who really care, the hypocrisy and hate-filled hijinks that is waged against blacks in Omaha (similar "games" are played at the expense of Latinos and Native Americans). I also know that tens of thousands of people from all over the nation, read this newspaper via the National Newspaper Publishers Association. And many of them have contacted me.

At any rate, I challenge the statistics and report of Nebraska being third in the nation in terms of violence against blacks. It simply doesn't add up, and as a social researcher of some repute, I've got to say that my fellow researchers should be castigated for the national lie that they've told, a lie that may generate grant money for the state and city, but it only brings hurt, harm and Excedrin headaches to Northsiders.

Let's use logic. Nebraska has about 1,700,000 people in it, and about 85,000 of them are black. That's about 5% of the entire population. And you're going to tell me that with all the banging going on in the Native American reservations, all the domestic squabbles that lead to death taking place in white suburbs, and all the dope-related murders going on in the Panhandle, that it's US that's doing all the killing?

Black-on-black homicides sound all the more ridiculous when you realize that we're only 5% of the population and that 95% of us are right here in Omaha, and that of that number, about 90% of us live in an 8-square mile area on the northeaster sector of the city. You're going to tell me that these paltry stats enable us to shoot this state through the rafters, all the way to number three, when:

- Dallas Texas is 26% black and Houston is 25% black. These cities stay in the news in terms of black-on-black and Latino-on-Latino homicides;
- Gary, Indiana is 84% black and Detroit is 83% black. Detroit is so bad that the movie "Robocop" parodied the violence there;
- What about cities with majority black populations? Are you going to tell me that Omaha has MORE black-on-black homicides than cities like (Birmingham, Jackson, New Orleans, Baltimore and Memphis?)
- You gonna tell me that Omaha has a greater incidence of black-on-black crime than jazz and gin crazy Kansas City, Missouri?

How could such amazing information be kept quiet for so long? It's easy: there's a grant out there somewhere and the state wants to cut it up between Lincoln and Omaha, the two cities with some semblance of blacks (Lincoln's is mostly transient because of the University athletes).

Blatant misconduct by political leadership, social services, the police establishment and the penal system. They had access to the information (if it existed) or had a hand in fabricating it, all along. There's no other way to look at it.
<u>(Cultural) Miasma</u>

Normally, this has to do with smog or some pollutant that messes up the atmosphere, which is why I specifically came up with and qualified the term as "cultural" miasma. In this case, it is defined as, "an influence or atmosphere that tends to deplete or corrupt; an atmosphere that obscures."

There is no doubt in anyone's mind that the most creative force in America is to be found in African-American communities. Everybody, from hicks and hillbillies to urban corporate types, copy our handshakes, music, terminology, fashion, and try to get their women to emulate our women's beauty (e.g., lips, rear-ends, and even attitude). Blacks in Nebraska are no different: despite our meager numbers we are still cutting edge when it comes to giving this otherwise cow town state what little "flavor" it's got.

How do you keep such creativity and influence "under control"? You really cannot, because there are Japanese, Chinese, and European kids copying and listening to whatever black kids in America do. But what you can do is lend a stigma to that creativity; in this case, associate that which is criminal and murderous with black youth. And that is what is being done, which is why far too many of those who are a part of the hip-hop generation associate the music and culture with violence and getting arrested.

You spread a "cultural miasma" over all that is black. Omaha is doing this only after spending millions of dollars in public relations money from 1960-1977 claiming that Omaha was "America's best kept secret." And then spent more money claiming that it was "diverse." But if you check out the hotel room brochures, the promotional literature, the tourism information and even the stuff they send out to black groups trying to get them to host their conferences here, there is nothing about black folks; nothing about the background and history that had us rivaling Kansas City; nothing about the Museum or Ernie or even Bob Gibson.

So it is a cultural miasma taking place: "an influence or atmosphere that tends to deplete or corrupt; an atmosphere that obscures." The one created by the majority to make invisible (through depletion by claiming we're killing each other at a national record setting level – as if they care) or corruption (stigmatizing an entire area – "North O" – as a den of sin, a community of killers – a veritable neighborhood of ne'er-do-wells.

Mayhem, Misconduct and the creation and circulation of a "Cultural Miasma." All of this tends to steer black folks into institutional arrangements that, in turn, generate money for the state. And if what I say is not true, I challenge ANY city, county or state official to debate me on the subject.

Next week: Why We Kill.

Part 3:
Oppositional Defiance Disorder, and the Northside: Reviewing, Refuting and Revising Some of the Classical "Black Homicide" Theories

How can a community of 60,000 catapult a state of 1,700,000 into the number 3 national position in black-on-black homicide? It cannot be done unless those controlling the system, the scholarship and the symptoms "rig" it that way. Following is how it's done.

"Culture of poverty." "Low self-esteem," "Tangle of pathology." These were some of the old theories that attempted to explain why black people tend to turn on one another. High population density was rarely explored, but we have since come to learn that areas that are crowded have a greater likelihood of violence: ask the Italians, the Latinos in el barrio, the Native Americans locked on reservations. Why should the ghetto be any exception?

Then there was Alvin Poussaint and his "why blacks kill blacks" theory that caught on like wildfire. I remember destroying him during a radio debate in Milwaukee back in 1990, when I caught him on the air skinning and grinning with these two Caucasian talk show hosts. I called in, they saw my name and knew who I was, but Poussaint didn't. After they greeted me (translation: kissing up so that I wouldn't dog them on my own hit morning show on a rival station), I went directly for Poussaint's jugular. Eventually, after I debunked his theories, lifestyle and attempts to appease Caucasian audiences, they cut me off the air.

Are our children becoming a generation of rump roasters, so intrigued with the thought of killing that they are willing to do it in order to get behind bars so that they can be sexually abused? Is home life so bad that even going to prison is better than the headaches and hassles of the home front? Is poverty so endemic and guaranteed that going to prison, at very least, offers three meals a day and someplace to sleep?

Here's ten (10) reasons, based on what I've observed, for the homicide rates in the black community (recall, however, in part 1 that it is the State of Nebraska's agencies that "drew first blood" by sitting back and exacerbating the conditions that led to the anti-social conduct being discussed here).

Young women having sex with young men who are members of rival gangs. This is the cause in far too many cases – most of the time it's the Southside (mainly T Street) and the North side (mainly 40th Street).

Blood feuds from prison lockup. Since most of us live in North Omaha, that's who we meet up with in detention. Problems get worse and once on the streets, that's where its eventually settled.

Avenging family "honor." Somebody messes with somebody's sister or daughter or mother, and "it's on."

Payback against a family member. Somebody does you wrong, and you go after somebody in their family, usually a totally innocent member, just to send a message.

Drug deals gone bad. Selling somebody some cut up "soap on a rope" and calling it crack can lead to a major problem when major money (or chump change in many cases) is involved. If you've been ripped off, you feel the need to send a message or else you've been "punked."

Snitches/Police Informants. Although many of the young ones say that, "It's tell or be told on," the fact is, nobody likes or trusts a snitch. Look at the record: that's the reason why so many of these kids are killing one another.

Gang initiations. That's right, and it's still taking place. These cowards drive by and have someone being initiated shoot somebody at random. They don't have to kill them – just shoot them. But being the poor shots that they are, death by drive by or murder by gang initiation far too often leads in an innocent person (or rival gang member) getting capped.

Manhood rites. In far too many communities, including suburban ones, having possession of a gun, owning one and threatening another person with one makes you a man. But what these kids don't realize is that whenever you pull a gun and you don't use it, you pave the way for somebody to come back on YOU.

Have gun, will travel. Many of these killings are bounties: "hits" on people paid for by other people. Some of the "other people" are folks who don't live anywhere near North Omaha and who can afford to put a bounty on some young black kid's head.

Self-defense. Some kids are just scared and pull a gun for self-protection not even meaning to use it. But they do (even by accident) and as the old folks teach us, "bullets don't have eyes."

The system and the social science is *rigged* against black youth. Now if these were *white kids* we were talking about, society would find some pseudo scientist (like Poussaint) to come up with an excuse to make the activity a "disease." So since that's the case, let me provide a legal defense for our kids, based on what's already on the books.

My research found this "disorder" known as "oppositional defiant disorder." It's described as "an on-going pattern of disobedient, hostile and defiant behavior toward authority figures which goes beyond the bounds of normal childhood behavior. People who have it may appear very stubborn." (Sounds like me!). But no, it goes much deeper because there are certain factors that have to be taken into account (as with all things).

As the research outlines it, The defiance has to interfere with the child's ability to function in school, home, or the community. But what if it is the community that is the problem because of the lack of support systems, impatient police officers and predators on every corner? Secondly, the defiance cannot be the result of another disorder (such as depression or anxiety or sleep disorder). Why couldn't it be? Our kids are lacking sleep as reliable studies have made clear. And third, "the child's behaviors have been happening for at least six months." Who came up with that time frame? Why couldn't have happened for one month under extreme conditions? How about two months under emergency conditions?

I write this to show how shaky these medical definitions and assessments are and can be. But if this is how they want it, and this is what it takes for our kids to be recognized in some way (so that we, as parents, can then take these "professionals" to task for creating and maintaining the conditions), then why can't these kids get paid? They're giving them what I call, "ding-a-ling ducats" (goon snaps) anyway for having attention deficit disorder. The parents are signing them up for disability so they can get a "Crazy check." So then, maybe if these kids get paid for "oppositional defiant disorder," they will be able to afford their own "three hots and a cot" and won't have to get arrested so they can to prison to get a place to eat and sleep!

So far I've identified the source, the symptoms and the systematic way black kids are used as fodder for prison. Next week, in Part 4, I offer SOLUTIONS. Stay tuned, social workers.

Part 4:
Solutions: Restoring Pride, Getting Paid and Empowering Our People – Preliminary Notes

I was a critical thinker, reader and writer long before those in power began instituting it in the schools as a part of the curriculum. As usual, when it comes to us, they are a day late and a dollar short. Whose fault is that? Ours, because we shouldn't be waiting on them to do "the right thing" by us, especially not after knowing their track record over the past, say, 400 years.

As a result of how I've directed my scholarly life, I have learned to use what is needed from those in power to benefit the context to which I owe my existence – the black community. But I never make the mistake of imitating the played out because, as Baraka (1967) once wrote, to do so would be "to imitate, and then not be able to stop, death."

M.A. Brennan is a brilliant (Anglo) community organizer and has written extensively on the subject. I am an urbanologist and I believe that what is good for the goose is not necessarily good for the gander. In this case, the basics for addressing issues in North Omaha should not be derived from what "outsiders' prescribe and/or dictate to us. This has been what has taken place on the part of the City, the County, the State and the so-called "grant providers." All of them, imitating the played out and then handing it down to us and our kids as "solutions."

I've always said that before you deal with our situation, make sure that what is being offered as a solution is really a solution and what is being posed as a problem is really a problem. When it comes to our kids and this black-on-black homicide thing, those in power have imposed their "bad guys" perception on the situation and all they can come up with is "lock 'em up." We need a foundation for the solutions I'll offer next week. So let's start with dealing with OUR reality, not someone else's manipulated manifestations of it.

Brennan writes of "community development" in the typical, ethnocentric, 'one size fits all' format. But as Chancellor Williams once said, "it is doubtful if even a DEVIL can write a book that is totally without truth." And so it goes: Brennan's concepts show us exactly what the problem is (though he poses it as solutions) and why we, as black people, keep winding up at the bottom of the socioeconomic ladder while outsiders prosper on our impoverished status.

Brennan writes: *"The formulation of goals and strategies is vital to the development of effective action and community development ... To begin this process, the forces shaping the community must be identified. Relevant issues can be the deficiencies and needs of the community, such as the need for improved infrastructure, service opportunities, housing, or jobs (needs assessments). While negative issues are often the focus of attention, this need not always be the case."*

Who are the "forces" shaping this community? Externally, it's the state, the city and the county. Internally, its leadership that is more beholden to those external forces than they are to the community (except during election time). This then, provides the ideological basis for where responsibility for these homicides squarely lie. Blame the parents if you want to; I say it's the people who create and maintain the conditions that are, in turn, conducive to the behavior that these same people claim to hate (but nevertheless earn a living off of). And these, in turn, become the "relevant issues" being deficiencies and needs. In a word: poverty pimps.

Continuing, Brennan cogently contends that, *"Plans for action often emerge out of an assessment of local skills, niche markets, and unique local conditions present (asset mapping)."* Here's where Brennan – and most other sunshine scholars – get the issue back asswards.

Black people are the most intelligent people on this planet. The thing is, our intelligence is what I call "creative intelligence." We set the trends, we adapt faster, we do things well and with flair, and we get the results we want. The only problem is creative intelligence is not what is measured in our schools: technical intelligence is. So the majority population is good at building robots and making elephants stand on their hind legs, but they have to copy from us to learn how to dress, think, shake hands, speak and appear "urbane." Our collective skill set is what others envy and crave – so they take advantage of our political powerlessness and simply STEAL it.

And guess who's watching: our kids. They see us too powerless to police ourselves, to handle our own enervating struggles, to speak out against injustice and defend them in schools. And they are ASHAMED -- and rightfully so. And like any person with an Anglo mind but a black body, we see that other person the same way an Anglo would: with disdain-and-how-dare-you. The result? BAM!!!

That's what "American Idol," "So You Think You Can Dance," "Making the Band," "The One," "Superstar USA" and so on, are all about: watering down true soul and talent (Black folks) and making it appear as if everyone can do what we do. When, in reality, what they do is find someone with blonde hair and blue eyes who can effectively COPY what they see us do, and that person beats out everybody else – even the originators of the talent! Our kids see this, and they lash out because they're frustrated and they have a collective case of abandonment issues.

Before solutions can come we have to understand the nature of the problem. Brennan suggests that, *"By assessing the relevant issues and assets and then ranking them in relation to importance and potential for achieving change, local groups can develop a vision and action agenda. This vision will serve as the general focus for action and community development efforts."* Such nastiness.

But in our case the problem is deciding on what the "relevant issues" are, what the "relevant assets" are, and then having the power to rank these without interference from outside (funding) sources. This has ALWAYS been our problem: not GETTING the white man, but getting him off our backs! Our kids see it – why can't YOU?

<u>Part 5:</u>
The Agenda For Autonomy: Restoring Pride, Getting Paid and Empowering Our People (Final Installment)

I've done just about all I can do except do it for you. I've laid it out, showed you the strategy that these outsiders have used, named names and challenged myself to dust off some of my old ideas and hand them to you on a silver platter. We deserve the recently reported spate of black-on-black homicides if what is in our power we do not do.

Stokely Carmichael and Dr. Charles V. Hamilton wrote in *Black Power: The Politics of Liberation in America* (1967), that "before a group can enter open society, it must first close ranks. Historians and African-American scholars remind us about how black people were never "debriefed" following more than three and a half centuries of enslavement and a number of African-American psychologists document the significance of the black holocaust to much of what is taking place in our behavior and thought processes today. Although he borrowed the statement from other scholars, Ali was essentially correct in his contention. Omaha is filled with people who repeat what they've heard and attempt to pawn the ideas off as their own.

Few have done anything about any of these issues, which is why the problems appear cyclical in nature and why "solutions" are offered only by those who can make money off of black adversity. It also explains the defeatist attitude and behaviors of many of our young people, with the final blow being a kind of "racial implosion," my explanation for the spate of black-on-black homicides that exist, not only in Nebraska, but across the nation.

The time has come for rockstrong solutions, many of which I proposed decades ago but now, with times being so tumultuous, perhaps naysayers and summertime strategists will pay heed and listen.

Following are some of the ideas that I have in the area of improving Omaha's central city (some of which I proposed back in 1993-94):

- Changing the name of Omaha Public Schools to the Omaha Independent School District; Create a new division, Office of Cultural Competency to address all issues dealing with race or ethnicity (formerly I called it a "cultural consultants commission")
- NAACP, Urban League and other North Omaha groups call a press conference and charge the state of Nebraska with genocide against North Omaha and abuse of Federal funds. Evidence can be provided by the Uhuru Sasa Research Institute
- Think tanks files a lawsuit/grievance against the government for providing Omaha with grants that the city has abused as those grants relate to providing for the poor
- Create a Task Force For the Creation of a North Omaha-based radio station, one that would specialize in: (1) talk and (2) jazz. The station would be 24 hours on the FM dial
- Request Learning Community funds to create The Ernie Chambers Institute for the Gifted and Talented (proposed 15 years ago)
- Think tank files a lawsuit/grievance documenting Douglas County's poor distribution system, one so bad that the state of Nebraska may have to consider monitoring it.
- Incorporating the area defined as "New Kemet," as an "urban municipality" and working to have Community Development Block Grants directly allocated to the area as an "urban experimental project" (bounded by Cuming on the south, Redick on the north, 60th on the west and 16th on the east.
- Create a North Omaha Development Advisory Board (NODAB) to monitor the city's allocation of funding in and around North Omaha
- Elect officials from that area (after dividing it up into five quadrants) to serve as a Council of Elders, giving North Omaha two sets of locally recognized officials
- Launch a program, "One Bank, One Community," divest from existing structures and begin a centralized one, or have existing banks bid on/vie for all North Omaha accounts. Demand that there be at least four North Omahans on the Board of Directors
- Create an Inner City Fundraising Council designed to generate funds for the area, to be deposited in a Central City Credit Union for internal development projects
- Create a "North Omaha Social Responsibility Fund," where each of the northside's 116 churches would donate $1,000 per year to a fund to

finance the proposed charter school, NODAB and the proposed radio station

- Begin working on the changing of street names after minority officials to include, but not be limited to: Sen. Ernie Chambers (Lake Street?), Dorothy Eure, Welcome Bryant, Buddy Hogan, Bertha Calloway, Charlotte Shropshire, Charlie Washington, Lerlean Johnson, Sara Rountree and others (they don't have to be dead – just great).
- Think tank creates a needs assessment survey to begin re-defining the general needs of the poorest residents and putting together a "MasterBudget" for submittal to the Federal Government
- Inner City Fundraising Council contacts Omaha based celebrities (Gabrielle Union, Buddy Miles, etc.) to put on concert to raise funds for ICFC projects and programs
- Inner City Fundraising Council organizes "TALON" – Tavern And Lounge Owners Network, to serve as an on-going source of funding for programs and jobs for youth at a rate of $100 per week apiece. Funds administered by Central City Credit Union
- Think tank, ICFC and CCCU create a grant proposal writing (development office) called "NEGRO" – Northside Empowerment Grant Research Organization to train and employ grantwriters to seek funding for central city programs and projects
- Organize the first-ever "LincOmaha Initiative Conference," seeking to unify Nebraska's two largest black communities.

It seems as if everybody is fighting for autonomy except black folks. What is autonomy? Autonomy is defined as, "*especially* : the right of self-government and/or, **2** : self-directing freedom and especially moral independence." We have the best pastors, ministers and preachers in the entire state of Nebraska, and they'll be the first to tell you. So we've got all the "religious" independence we need. But religion and morality, as Christians show every day, are oftentimes two different things.

We need some moral independence and that begins with defining what's right and what's wrong: if you think our kids are wrong for killing each other, then show them something better. I have GIVEN YOU something, over the past six weeks, that will do just that.

To put it mildly, North Omaha deserves way better than they've been getting. I've witnessed it since 1977, and things are much different now – for the worse, that is. Come on, if I know it, you know it. If we pull together and deal with our area as what is it – a micropolis – we can make things better. Outsiders only want us for one thing: our impoverished zip codes. That's why THEY get the snaps and we're left with our naps. History proves me right.

We can petition the County, the State and the government to bring immediate attention to our collectively hellish plight. No one would suspect such a thing from Omaha, Nebraska. And while that's going on, we do our autonomy thing and start naming some streets, some buildings and some parks in our own image and interests. We don't need the City Council's approval: look what happened a few years back with Chambers Park. This is OUR community and THEY have made that clear. As I wrote last week, we don't want to get the white man – we just want to get him off our backs.

There's a group called the Midlands Bar Association (notice they make no associate or identification with race). But they're supposed to be a group of African-American attorneys. Oh, really? Well then, kick down some pro bono assistance on some of these empowering ideas. Sometimes we may be wrong – but many times, we will be RIGHT.

I've watched TV and movies enough (and studied law) to know that in order to find somebody guilty of a crime you need to establish motive, means and opportunity. Flip that to this call for the need for autonomy. North Omahans have the motive (systemic neglect of the area), the means (some 50,000-plus strong residents who are tired of the same ol' same ol' – which is why our kids are playing "wild, wild, west"), and opportunity: as Jesse once said, "nobody can save us for us from us but us."

I've laid it out for you and never fear – I will be ego-tripping about it in the days, weeks, months and years ahead. If someone out there with the time, energy, brains and guts can implement any of these ideas, North Omaha's context can be altered, and the self-destructive actions of our children will diminish (not even THEY want to destroy an area that has a positive future). Each of these ideas comes with its own separate 2-page strategic plan and timeline. Let's see who, out there, has the guts to contact me and get the ball rolling.

CONCLUSION

It has now been just over seven and years since the appearance of the World-Herald articles and my relevant response. What has taken place since that time?

Not much. Henry Cordes still has his job and the cops are still screwing up. In mid-June of 2017, two cops – both black – killed a Native American suspect with a taser:

> The Oklahoma man who died after Omaha police shocked him
> with a stun gun suffered from mental illness and had been
> wandering, lost, in Omaha for a day after being kicked off an
> interstate bus, his family says.Zachary N. Bearheels, 29, died early
> Monday after Omaha police used a Taser on him during a
> confrontation at the Bucky's gas station at 6003 Center St … Her
> son was bipolar and schizophrenic, she said.

When a civilian shot a Native child and a black man in the back in 1996, I acted and shut down the Kwik Shop where that white boy worked. I organized Native Americans and we boycotted, in knee deep snow, and took away that store's liquor license. When the store could no longer sell 40 ounce beers, its top revenue generator, they shut down. Two months later the store was torn to the ground. This is the kind of action that I'm talking about and that I'm known for: not the mealy-mouthed milquetoast mutterings of people like Councilman Ben Gray, so-called leaders like Willie Barney, Willie Hamilton, Dell Gines and others, or the Sunday shouting matches of these hallelujah hucksters, the black ministers.

I don't believe in prayer vigils. These negroes have been praying for decades and the only thing they've gotten is air sandwiches. And yet they keep on thinking that times are going to get better simply because their god, the white man, tells them so.

As for the death of Bearheels,

> She said she asked officers to take him to the bus station or a crisis center. Her son was frightened of police but was accustomed to going to a crisis center, she said, because that's what police in Oklahoma do. Omaha police, she said, told her they couldn't place him under emergency care because he wasn't a threat to himself or others. Ten minutes later, they requested an ambulance after a Taser use. The man was taken to the Nebraska Medical Center with CPR in progress. He was pronounced dead on arrival.

On-going buffoonery, backwardness and misfeasance. He was dead on arrival because of the police, plain and simple. They should be sued, but how is the family going to get justice from an un-just legal system? After all, this is Omaha, and it is protected by a racist media, led by reporters like Henry Cordes and Omaha World Herald fluff masters like Mike Kelly. All North Omaha has is me and my award-winning newsletter, and most of my kudos come from national sources. These people read and enjoy what I say, but they ain't gonna do a damn thing. Bearheels is dead and it seems like nobody gives a shit. Once again black people, going against the grain of the poem by Dylan Thomas, continue to "go gently into that good night."

Buffoonery reigns in the Omaha Police Division and this has been the case for over a century. The incompetent redneck joins the force, gets fatter and slower, and knows he can gun down and/or kill citizens and get away with it. State Senator Ernie Chambers has well documented these incidents.

Typical of the lie- and excuse-laden explanations can be found in the following passage:

> "Unfortunately, the (Omaha Police Department's) policy does not have clear written guidelines for use of a Taser on people experiencing a mental health crisis, people using medication to address mental health issues, or people under the influence of drugs or alcohol," said Danielle Conrad, executive director of the ACLU of Nebraska. "This is a reminder that Tasers are lethal weapons and that they should only be used as a last resort."

No clear written guidelines on the use of a Taser. Forgetting for two decades to submit homicide stats. On-going examples of slipups on the job and cop cars running into each other. The Omaha Police Division makes the Keystone Cops look like the Avengers.

Henry Cordes – a dead ringer for the nerd Neil Goldman from "Family Guy" – wrote an article that was approved by a committee of fellow racists. And that is how the Omaha World Herald operates. No black reporters and other than localite Sibyl Myers who is now deceased, even the "negroes" they brought in didn't last long and were more screwed up in the head (read: Tony Moton) than many of the white reporters.

Let me then repeat myself from an opening statement on Cordes: "People like this reporter Cordes specialize in one thing: fluff pieces supporting white institutions and the usual stigma-laden reports from North Omaha, although he doesn't have the guts to venture into the area. He's a coward for the most part, but this is par for the course when it comes to Omaha news reporters and the police: they arrive in time to take pictures of the bodies and to scrape up the bodies, respectively."

<u>"Benign Encroachment: The "Fair Deal" Project</u>

INTRODUCTION

For the past century, North Omaha – the area of the city where the overwhelming majority of the black people in the state of Nebraska reside – has been treated like an abused step-child when it came down to the fair allocation of city services, political representation and neighborhood/community development. While many, including this writer, have attempted to bring attention to the situation, Omaha has lived up to its one-time slogan of being "America's best kept secret." Because the black community is so small (60,000 people) and the state is so rurally situated, even the city of Omaha can be overlooked when Federal decision makers have the likes of New York, Los Angeles, Chicago, Detroit,

Philadelphia and other mega cities to deal with. When one things of "urban problems," the city of Omaha is not one of the metro areas that comes to mind.

This paper is a response to yet another "announcement" regarding "attempts" to "help North Omaha." The more that is written when people see these kinds of atrocities being repeated, the more likely it is that someone will one day come along and put all the pieces to the puzzle together and see how the city of Omaha, despite its low ranking in terms of total population, has nevertheless devised ploy after ploy to generate federal money based on black poverty and then, once the money arrives, use those funds to annex adjacent towns (to increase its size and therefore increase the amount of the free grant checks) and generally create loan funds and suburban leisure activities, riverfront development attractions, and downtown expansion.

North Omaha's part in this scenario is that North Omaha is in the perfect geographical position to expand on white leisure activity. An area that has long time been the segregated bane of the white establishment, North Omaha is nevertheless the area with the best flat land, the nicest avenues and boulevards, optimum proximity to the Missouri River and minutes away from downtown, where there are more than 25,000 jobs.

One mayor, in preparing for the merger of downtown and North Omaha (even as black people in North Omaha are gradually being located to the northwestern sector of the city), dubbed the area "No-Do" – as in "North Downtown." This ludicrous slang was followed up with the construction of a huge baseball stadium, several yuppie-oriented night clubs, and condominiums --- all on the border of what was once North Omaha and Omaha's once-dying downtown. In addition, Creighton University, which lies on the southern fringe of the black community, has done all that it can to up the security in the area, buy up a mini-mall that doubles as a health center for its students, and generally create a "fortress" on the fringe. So comfortable are the combined efforts of the city and Creighton that white coeds can now job down through the heart of the black community and know that they have nothing to fear because behind them stand Creighton security, the Omaha Police Department and who knows what else.

This paper explains the reason for the "Fair Deal Urban District," reasoning that goes much deeper than professed claims of "wanting to help the area." The concept of what constitutes a "fair deal" is linked to former President Franklin Roosevelt's "New Deal" and while the two may sound light years apart, there is a connection in terms of the black response to Roosevelt in terms of launching "buy black" campaigns and on-going "meetings" that would take place to organize and clean up the community, as well as meet to discuss politics.

This paper also charges that there exists, "placation and long-term takeover strategies," facts that perhaps exist in all cities where there is a centralized black population that is in need of being disbursed. This paper documents decades of various "plans" and "programs" that were used as a smokescreen to slowly encroach on the black community. You will see that aiding and abetting the city in these plans was the major newspaper, the Omaha World Herald, continuing to carry water for the system in exchange for "exclusives."

In the case of the newspaper, I address what I view as "words and symbols" that set the table for the encroachment that I allege. These antics could not continue on time and time again were they not rubber-stamped with articles singing their praises, editorials claiming that "better days lie ahead" and so on. All of this documented in past "black papers" that I have submitted to the newspaper, the city administration and Omaha's leadership to no avail.

Having provided context, I then delve into my assessment of the proposed "Fair Deal Urban District," along with an alleged umbrella plan known as the $1.43 billion "North Omaha Village Revitalization Plan" (which was announced in the summer of 2011). The fact is, had the city of Omaha properly spent the more than $200 million that it has received since 1975 on the North Omaha area, there would already be a thriving area where the ghetto is now located. Furthermore, how can we expect the city to spend almost a *billion and a half dollars* on North Omaha when they wouldn't do the right thing with the $200 plus *million* that they already had?

THE ORIGINAL "NEW DEAL": IMPACT ON NORTH OMAHA

> Franklin Roosevelt, in his second Inaugural Address, told a rain-soaked crowd, "The test of our progress is not whether we add more to the abundance of those who have much; it is whether we provide enough for those who have too little." (quoted in Herbert, B. (2010). Shhh, don't say "poverty." In Paula S. Rothenberg (Ed.). *Race, Class, and Gender in the United States.* New York, New York: Worth Publishers (p. 324)

When Roosevelt first came out with his Fair Deal plan, some people in the community called it a "dirty deal." William Allen White, editor of the *Gazette* of Emporia, Kansas, wrote in 1933 that, The New Deal was creating "a great political machine centered in Washington." In 1935, Senator Huey Long of Louisana, and originator of the Share the Wealth Society, stated that, "[U]nless we do share our wealth, unless we limit the size of the big man so as to give something to the little man, we can never have a happy or a free people...." He added that he, felt that Roosevelt's New Deal was too conservative and moving too slowly. Even former president Herbert Hoover got into the act and during a speech on June 10, 1936 said, "Either we shall have a society based upon ordered liberty and the initiative of the individual, or we shall have a planned society that means dictation, no matter what you call it or who does it. There is no halfway ground."

And in 1937, columnist Dorothy Parker called Roosevelt's plan to "pack" the Supreme Court with his supporters a step toward dictatorship and added, "If the American people accept this last audacity of the President without letting out a yell to high heaven, they have ceased to be jealous of their liberties and are ripe for ruin. This is the beginning of a pure personal government."

Roosevelt's "New Deal" was a sign to black people to band together socially and economically. Even in Omaha, such an idea was grasped and transformed into example upon example of operational unity.

Then there was the Fair Deal Café, which was a key cog in the "unification of negroes" in the River City. This was a place that black people came to socialize, especially the elders. You could go there and sit over coffee all day long, and the owner, Charlie Hill, would join in every now and then. It was almost like a family atmosphere, as a number of his children and other people's children worked as waitresses there at one time or another. It was the kind of café that you used to find in almost any black community you went to. Integration came and destroyed many of them, but the Fair Deal was able to stay around. When I ran for mayor back in 1997, I used the Fair Deal as the site of my press conference because I knew all this history about it, and it was good public relations for the café.

Then it was sold to a woman, Tommie Wilson and her daughter, who have never really had the black community's best interests at heart. As NAACP president Wilson set black progress back for years with her inane public comments and inaction. After she bought the café, it floundered and eventually it was closed. Now here comes the white man to use that as a reason to come into the community and bamboozle black people, as if they (those in power) haven't had more than a century to extend a "fair deal" to North Omaha's blacks.

But back to the 1930s, which were a time of the Great Depression, and blacks believed that some of the New Deal programs would help them. They got, from the New Deal, the same insulation, security and solace that the Fair Deal would later provide. As Moore (1971) pointed out,

> Hundreds of individual campaigns such as 'Don't Buy Where You Can't Work' appeared in the black communities of Washington, D.C., Chicago, New York, Cleveland, Los Angeles and Omaha, Nebraska. In Omaha, Jaspar Cole of 2928 North 25th Street secured race employment at Bushler Brothers Market of 24th and Lake Streets by this type of campaign (p. 3).

The "don't buy where you can't work campaign" was somewhat successful in Omaha because it caught white people by storm. These signs alone, even without militant black people shouting for equality, prompted many of the white businesses to begin hiring black women as elevator operators and, for sure, it opened up the packing houses and meat packing plants even more than they already were.

By June of 1940, the Omaha Star newspaper continued the doctrine of "don't buy where you can't work." An (error-filled) editorial in the June 7th edition made the point quite convincingly:

> During the existence (sic) of the OMAHA STAR its Editorial (sic) policy has been to develop thought proving (sic) editorials in which to a large measure, they have been written on (sic) conditions as found in Omaha, seen through the unbias (sic) eye of the Editor (sic) of this publication. It has been ours to receive through the mail, letters commenting on many of the pertinent questions written upon (sic), all of whom (sic) have been welcomed by the Editorial (sic) staff of this paper.
>
> As we near the close of our second year of service to the reading public in Nebraska and to those of 21 other states of these United States, we bring to you a subject that we feel is vital to all Black America. "Don't spend your money Where (sic) YOU Can't Work." Because of the economic condition in which we, Black America, find ourselves, it is the belief of this publication that some action to clear up this condition should be taken. It is further the belief of this the voice of the people that the most effective way through which we are to get results, is through the harnessing of our dollars spent in such a way to demand respect.
>
> Many of you, perhaps, do not realize the vast amount of money that is spent by us as a group. That this fact might be brought to you, more vividly, we shall take Omaha as an example with its 16,000 Negro inhabitants. It is obvious (sic) that an average of one dollar and twenty-five cents is either spent on or by each member of our group each day. That being true $20,000 per day $600,000 per month $7,200,000 per year passes from or (sic) group to those engaged in some form of business periodically.
>
> Thus it is on the basis of this vast amount of money spent daily, monthly, and yearly, that we ask you, Black America, to consider our slogan "Make Your Dollar Count By Refraining From Spending the same where you are denied the opportunity to work." If this you will only do, we can assure a change in employment policies especially in locations like

North 24th Street, where we constitute at least 85 percent of
the buying public.

Black America we beseech each of you to cease crying
about those of Omaha and especially on North 24th street who
refuses (sic) you employment and to the contrary use that
energy in informing yourself and others as to the slogan that
should be the by word of every black American. "Don't Spend
Your Money Where You Can't Work." We ask for Action!
(all punctuation original).

The previous article appeared just over seventy years ago, and it is evidence
that the courage and conviction of black people was at a higher level then, when
there were so few (16,000 compared with 60,000 today in 2012). But this editorial
was not the end of it by any means. Black people back then also had another
quality that blacks in North Omaha today also seem short on: perseverance.

The previous editorial was followed up the following week with a front page
editorial, this one featuring the Omaha Negro Chamber of Commerce. Following is
the full text of that June 14, 1940 article:

Calling not for violent but intelligent action, the Omaha
Negro Chamber of Commerce, beseech (sic) every Black
American in Omaha to join in a united effort with the chamber
to improve its social, economic, and civic status. You are being
urged to consider seriously our slogan for the year 1940-41,
"Don't Spend Your Money Where You Can't Work" and then
act accordingly. The questions may arise, how can this be
done? In an explanatory answer, we call your attention to the
following facts:

The Jew receives the respect from others, because
through unity he has built a financial empire, the foreign
element receives the respect because through unity he has built
a political front line defense. You Black America, the largest
minority group in Omaha, can if you only will, gain the respect
of building up a consumer's economic cloc (sic).

It is you here in Omaha who spend $20,000 per day,
$600,000 pr month, and $7,200,000 per year, the largest
consuming (sic) market in Omaha in ratio of (sic) population.
This being true, when and if you will use the power which you
have in hand, and so harness the dollar you spend daily in
accordance to the slogan as adopted by the Chamber, we shall
find our group being accorded the respect as is tended all their
American citizens, such action will mean that as we go in to
our neighboring stores we will be served by Black hands. Our
boys and girls shall be able to find employment in stores and

business establishments on N. 24th street and elsewhere, where we constitute from 75 to 95 per cent of the patronage.

This educational campaign will be launched on the evening of June 29, the date set for the annual meeting of the Chamber at which time the new elected officers: S. Edward Gilbert, president; Mr. J.D. Lewis, vice pres.; Mr. A. Hancock, secretary; Mr. A. Hines assistant secretary; Dr. Milton E. Johnson, treasurer; and Mr. Wendell Thomas, chairman of the executive committee; will be duly installed for the ensuing year (Omaha Star, 1940: 1).

While standing up for the community and working to get them jobs, the *Omaha Star* newspaper was also acting in its own best self interests. The newspaper felt it deserved advertisement from area businesses and that the numbers black people represented in terms of both population and money being spent demonstrated that the community was deserving of having a message geared directly toward black residents.

A June 28, 1940 editorial in the *Omaha Star* was titled, "Merchants Tell Us Your Story" says it all:

Members of the Omaha Star staff have been queried continually about the lack of advertising from some of the popular stores in Omaha. These people 16,000 of them are wondering why it is that even though they spend thousands of dollars in these stores monthly they do not know about bargains and special sales through the Omaha Star. One of our readers said only a short while ago that he missed a wonderful buy in fall suits at one of the leading men's clothing stores simply because he heard not one word about it in the Omaha Star and hence did not know about it.

Many such instances have been called to our attention. Naturally the best way to contact Negro buyers is through the medium that reaches them and them alone. The Negro press has the greatest trader interests for the Negro and naturally it becomes the best medium of advertising that is, if the merchants expect more Negro business.

The Negroes of Omaha have a combined buying power, based on $1.25 per person, per day of $20,000 … $600,000 per month, and $7,200,000 per year, and these stores complain that they are not getting this Negro business. There can be only one reason for not getting this business. They do not ask for it. They can hardly expect to get this business each week by not advertising some journal that directly reaches the Negro public.

> This being true the Omaha Star invites each and every
> merchant to tell us your merchandise story where we can find
> it – in our publication (Omaha Star, 1940: 3).

In Omaha during the Depression, white men were shining shoes, waiting tables, driving trucks, doing scavenger work, digging ditches and doing other jobs formerly held by blacks as their own. The Family Welfare Association reported blacks consisted of about 25% of their cases and the Salvation Army also reported a black case load of 12% of their total cases which indicated this economic pressure on Negroes in Omaha (Moore, 1971: 3; Kerns, 1932: 26; Sullenger & Kerns, 1931: 14).

Despite being impoverished financially, the spirit of blacks in North Omaha remained rock strong, and black women were no exception:

> On June 23, 1932, the Omaha Housewives' League
> was formed to carry on a relentless drive of women to assist
> Negroes in their efforts to achieve economic recognition. The
> League was a branch of the national organization, with
> headquarters in New York City … The main goal of the
> Omaha Housewives' League was to create as many jobs for
> blacks as possible by purchasing a required amount of items
> each day from a black-owned store in the community. This
> intelligent direction of spending power of the League and
> closer cooperation among blacks in business created a number
> of permanent jobs (Moore, 1971: 3-4).
>
> In 1933, six northside stores got together in an attempt
> to overcome the difficult times and created "Square Deal
> Stores," which "endeavored to give first quality food for less
> money by means of group purchasing and stimulate an interest
> in all business conducted by blacks in Omaha" (Moore, 1971:
> 4).

Courage and conviction of the many has now, over the years, been decimated to the self-serving actions of the few. Today, perhaps the masses are satisfied, but also most of them are aware of the con games that have been run on North Omaha and who the players are. Many are just glad to see some blacks being involved, even when those blacks are working with outside interests to divide up the community.

Clearly, the creation of the Fair Deal Urban District is in no way as expansive or as favorable to black people and the poor as the New Deal. And this is precisely my point: the people who control the power to name things also have the power to impact on those who do not live in Omaha and are therefore not privy to the kinds of callousness, the degree of degradation, that they tend to heap upon the heads of North Omaha residents on a regular basis. I have long chronicled some of these shady shenanigans and were they not so dangerously dastardly, they would be laughable.

Following, in the midst of cheers and people screaming "hip, hip, hooray" are my analyses and criticism of just one more "scam" being run on North Omaha in an effort to build leisure activities for suburban whites who will be re-taking the inner city while at this time, right now, duping black people into thinking that "all this" is for them.

NORTH OMAHA: PLACATION AND LONG-TERM TAKEVOER STRATEGIES

It has been both said and written that, "short-term pleasure yields long-term pain." Black people in North Omaha have apparently not learned that yet, even though the history is replete with example upon example. The city power structure, aided by the major newspaper (which controls most of the newspapers in the state) have duped and bamboozled North Omahans and their leadership for more than a century. The philosophy of black people seems to be, "if the white man said it, then it must be true." A true concern about and commitment to North Omaha by the city power structure, past or present, is anything BUT the truth.

Recall, if you will, that almost 50 years ago to the day -- in September of 1962 -- Omaha's central city was the site of 60 percent of the community's real estate valuation. With this in mind, the "takeover plans" began. Stevens (1981) wrote, *"Yet under their confident exteriors, downtown businessmen felt threatened by the physical decline of the inner city and by the emergence of suburban shopping centers on the western outer fringes of Omaha. In September 1962, Chamber of Commerce president Marvin G. Schmid announced a major campaign to upgrade the physical plant of the central city."*

This is the role that the major newspaper plays in these kinds of plans. Although change for the area continues to always be, "announced," apparently no one follows through. The people get happy, the planners have a good laugh, and then sit back and nothing gets done.

In 1972, courtesy of another "grant," came a neo-colonialist idea where those who looked like the North Omaha resident – many who even lived among them – would be "used" to manipulate the land and the housing thereby making it easier for outside incursions into the area. The group was given the name, "North Omaha Community Development:"

> The first incorporation of an organization named North Omaha
> Community Development was in 1972. It was an outgrowth of
> a grant received by the City of Omaha from the United States
> Department of Housing and Urban Development (HUD). The
> objective of the grant was to prepare a community
> development plan … Pursuant to a provision in the grant for
> citizen participation, the City made an effort to insure resident
> input … Eventually a group emerged from this City initiated
> effort and incorporated as North Omaha Community
> Development (NOCD, no date).

The city made no "effort to ensure resident input." What the city did was begin hand picking which few residents would be given a chance to play the role of "head nigger in charge" and essentially be the eyes and ears of the city administration, reporting back to the Planning Department on a regular basis. This is what took place then, in 1972, and this is what is taking place now, in 2012.

The NOCD organization membership went around claiming that it would "change" the area. Then NOCD-president George Garnett said in early 1980, *"24th and Lake Street has been the center of business, the spiritual center of the community. If that area can be revitalized, it will have a ripple effect and it will be easier to turn the rest of the community around."*

Either Garnett was incredibly stupid or he was the biggest race traitor that blacks in Omaha had seen since Jericho Honore led a bunch of black students at the University of Nebraska at Omaha to "sit in" on the Chancellor's office (thereby getting everybody arrested and "marking," for the establishment, who the rabble-rousers on campus were).

The fact of the matter is, Garnett and NOCD did little, if anything. The same principle regarding the "ripple effect" that Garnett spoke of earlier also works in two other ways. First of all, it can work in reverse: if you can kill 24th Street, then you destroy the rest of the community as well. Simply look at 24th and Lake Street now and ask a question: does it look better now than it did in 1975 when the City of Omaha first began receiving millions from the Federal government? The answer is a resounding, "no."

And it can work in a way known as "chaos theory," where the smallest ripple can have an unpredictable impact many miles away. As North Omaha was being taken over by the powers that be, the simpletons making the decisions were learning from other cities like Denver, Kansas City, Des Moines, as well as smaller cities around Nebraska were watching what Omaha was doing to its "low-income people" and also trying to copy it. As Omaha goes, so goes Nebraska. And even though Omaha has the only real black population in the state, there are small pockets elsewhere – Lincoln, Grand Island, Bellevue – that are perhaps also in need of being controlled, and don't forget the growing Nebraska Latino populations and of course, the Native Americans on the various reservations.

In January of 1981, the *Omaha World Herald* ran an editorial titled, "North Omaha Skies Brighten," claiming that the freeway would bring in businesses and jobs. Did it? No. Later in the same year, 1981 a "study" by a Chicago group called Real Estate Research Corporation (RERC) suggested that the Blue Lion Center be the "business hub" of North Omaha and promised that if this happened, new business would appear. Has it? No.

In March of 1982, seven years after the City of Omaha had begun receiving millions in CDBG monies, a 12-member committee was formed to study revitalization "and crime" in the area claiming at the time that the 24th and Lake intersection was *"undergoing a facelift, including landscaping and renovation of two vacant buildings into specialty shops, entertainment facilities and office space."* Where is all this?

Later, in 1994, there would come claims of $50 million being "earmarked" for North Omaha, various "committees" being set up and promises being made by bank after bank. These tricks and traps continue on to this very day. And the list goes on and on.

In 1997 a "Race Commission" was formed to deal with problems in a number of areas across the city. When it came to economic development, the following recommendation was made:

> … Community based organizations (CBOs) that have
> minority advancement as their stated mission will be
> contacted to create a pool of potential entrepreneurs …

For the most part, CBOs have no power. They are nonprofit corporations that rely on grants and donations to survive. How then, are they going to talk of "minority advancement" without being dependent upon "outsiders" for that advancement? As for creating a pool of potential entrepreneurs, whether or not they have the potential is not the question: the question is, who in the business community is going to be supportive and assist them in actualizing that potential? Who in the city or county ranks is going to put aside their racism and allow black potential in North Omaha to blossom into fruition?

Placation tactics, every single one of them.

To "placate" or "pacify" means to "appease." Just because a population that has been deprived for over a century is not accustomed to being treated fairly gives you no right to take advantage of that fact by coming in and feeding them air sandwiches and hope pudding and calling it "empowerment," or "community development," or in this case, "village revitalization."

These and related tactics appear to come out of the woodwork every other year but when they do, the approach may differ but the end result is the same: keep black people smiling, keep so-called "negro leadership" convinced that they are actually involved (ask them questions during interviews as if they really count), and make sure that white developers get paid and the free grant money from the Federal government keeps pouring in.

WORDS AND SYMBOLS SET THE TABLE

The method, as I stated earlier, is not a new one. In fact, it represented what now, in retrospect, appears to be an historical tendency, documented in a work written in 1971 called, *Odyssey: Journey Through Black America*. In one segment, long-time Omaha dentist Earle Person had this observation:

> When the whites put together their downtown area, their slogan was: "Can do." We [blacks in Omaha] saw that the slogan for the Near North Side was: "Won't do." The prime movers just say, "Well, we'll try a few little things, form a committee, call in an outside research organization, make a study." And they do survey after survey after survey, and all of them get stuck away in some file … (Selby & Selby, 1971: 290).

There were always people who could see what was taking place: Omaha was willing to give money to outside interests to "tell" them what to do in the area of planning and neighborhood development. The fact is, the money that they were using, at least a huge amount of it, was money from the Community Development Block Grant funds that came to the city each year to address black impoverishment. And yet very little of that money was spent improving the black community.

Twelve years after the previous article appeared, as a graduate student at the University of Nebraska Omaha, I wrote somewhat of a follow-up on the claims made by Person in an "Another Point of View" letter. My opinion piece initially appeared in the *World Herald* and was then reprinted a week later on the front page of the *Omaha Star*. At that time I wrote, in part,

> … Money is flowing out of the city at a time when Mayor Boyle claimed he would be seeking to bring business in. How can he – or anyone – do that when the basis of any successful venture is, indeed, an environment where there is economic stability? And how can we become economically stable when we do not use our own internal resources during

> fact-finding or other types of endeavors? (Stelly, 1982: 7;
> Stelly, 1982: 1).

And,

> … while the city and others seem content with spending
> money on outside consultants and analysts, Omahans face
> an economic crunch which manifests itself in a myriad of
> ways. (Stelly, 1982: 7; Stelly, 1982: 1).

The "Omahans" that I was writing about and concerned most with were the black residents of the Northside. Two years prior to my article appearing, a conservative member of the Omaha City Council, Tim Rouse, was able to describe – and in this case also sum up – what had taken place in and around North Omaha in a 1980 *Omaha World Herald* editorial:

> City Councilman Tim Rouse, who alleged that the Veys
> administration has neglected blacks in Northeast Omaha,
> clearly doesn't think the question is settled. Rouse said – and
> King reported – that the black neighborhood in Northeast
> Omaha needs more than an equal amount of effort because of
> 20 to 30 years of neglect (Omaha World Herald, 1980: 4).

Since the preceding article appeared in 1980, it is clear that what had taken place in North Omaha was the result of much more than just "20 to 30 years of neglect." And it should be noted that Rouse didn't care about black people – he was running for Mayor and wanted to sound as if he did.

At about the same time, in an article written by Omaha World Herald reporter Sibyl Myers (the only black on the staff at that time), it was "predicted" that,

> In the next six months to a year, there will be a marked change
> in the appearance of North Omaha, the new executive director
> of North Omaha Community Development, Inc., [George
> Garnett] said. And in five years, North Omaha will have 'a
> new facelift that not only will make the area more viable, but
> also will make people not recognize it' (Omaha World Herald,
> no date).

Garnett saw the writing in the wall and, during his frequent meetings with various city officials, he learned, no doubt, about their plans to invade the black community by pushing the indigenous population further and further northwest. A

World-Herald editorial, titled "Skies Over North Omaha Brighten," continued to promise jobs and "development" to the area by using vague terms like "appears," and "should" so as not to make an actual promise that would have to be fulfilled:

> Last August, it was noted editorially that there was a surge of activity to revitalize Omaha's North Side … Omaha also appears finally ready to get on with building the extension of the North Freeway and the Arthur C. Storz Expressway to Eppley Airfield. This should offer the better transportation needed to provide development and jobs in the area. As the new year begins, the skies over North Omaha do, indeed, look brighter for 1981 and the years to follow (Omaha World Herald, 1981: 4).

More promises of jobs in the area. That was in 1981 – just over 30 years ago. Where are they? So to make that unsubstantiated claim to the media, with no evidence or projections to back it up, is par for the course in Omaha. The same thing goes for development; the people who put the freeway in had the nerve to promise area businesses that the freeway would bypass that indeed, the roadway would actually help! Even with the addition of two exists along the way, black business died and more than fifty units of affordable housing was torn down to make way for a freeway whose real purpose was to get white folks from west Omaha to the airport as rapidly as possible.

THE FAIR DEAL URBAN DISTRICT: ABRA-KADABRA!

I have been on the city's trail for more than two decades, exposing them in front of the entire community, black and white, in reference to their abuse of Federal funds and their neglect of North Omaha. I have proven, through rock-solid research, that the "programs" and "projects" that they continue to concoct are nothing short of pitiable.

The most recent debacle being pawned off as development, is the Fair Deal Urban District. I don't like it, not even the name of it, because of the following reasons:

1. Fair deal is a double entendre. The name was about the good prices on the food.
2. By calling if Fair Deal urban District, the far-reaching implication (read: marketing) is that the area is the result of a "fair deal" when nothing could be further from the truth.

3. If you take the word "fair" and look it up, it means without blemish or, more clearly, light in complexion. That is the goal of those in power: to erase black people's presence from the area and shift it from being "of color" (read: blemished) to "fair."
4. In cards a fair deal is one that goes by the rules. The city's relationship with North Omaha has been anything but "fair" and in fact, there are a plethora of examples of the city "dealing from the bottom of the deck"
5. The Fair Deal Café was a place for black unity, for people to talk about what racism, segregation and the City of Omaha was doing to them. Very few, if any, white folks were in on these conversations. Now they have the gall to wait until the place has closed down, gone through mismanagement and attempt to revive it by applying the name of a place of solitude and planning to a "project" that is rife with scheming and perversity.

On _____, the *Omaha World Herald* published an article by Cindy Gonzalez, titled, "North Omaha's Old Fair Deal Cafe is Center of $12.2 Million Plan." The article begins, thusly:

> Omaha officials broke ground today on a $12.2 million project to revive a two-square-block area that includes part of the historic North 24th Street commercial corridor. The new "Fair Deal Urban District" will replace blighted properties and empty lots with apartment housing for seniors, single homes for families and an arts center (Gonzalez, 2012).

These articles always talk about the developers and city officials "reviving" an area but they seldom provide context on what happened to the area that led to its "demise." To the tune of more than $200 million to date, the city has received money from the government to repair North Omaha, to upgrade housing, provide jobs and social services and to make it no longer a "pocket of poverty." That money has been squandered on other parts of the city. Instead, the city opts to purchase and upgrade buildings for itself, so much that now major city structures occupy the four corners of "24th and Lake Streets," which was the "cultural hub" of the area where the Fair Deal is located.

The area died because of the failure of the city to fairly disperse resources and services, opting instead to sit back and watch while crime escalated which, of course, meant more grants: Weed and Seed, Project Safe Neighborhoods, Project Triggerlock, etc. The City of Omaha has spent billions of (free) Federal money claiming that they wanted to deal with the issues and problems of North Omaha. The issues and problems today, in 2012, are *worse* than they were in 1977 when I first arrived in what was a bustling and audacious black community.

The "blighted properties" and "empty lots" that are described above have a history, and their current status is evidence and provides remnants of that history, one saddled with racial strife, white segregation and responsive race riots. Here is a key fact that the city and the media always tend to overlook; the fact that Charlie Hill was in charge of code enforcement during those days. An August 31, 1980 article in the *Omaha World Herald* lays the blame squarely at Hill's door:

> "[Charlie] Hill… said Omaha's condemnation proceedings that start with complaints. There is no plan for routine inspection of buildings to ensure compliance with building codes, Hill said. As for condemnations … it appears to him the city may have been overly diligent in condemning property in North Omaha. Many buildings probably could have been saved with effort toward rehabilitation, he said, but instead they were condemned and torn down."

There has been a "tendency," as we can see – twice is a coincidence and three times is a trend. Omaha had been destroying housing in the urban core for decades. By condemning the buildings in the area, you can condemn the area that the buildings are in, and if you condemn that area, you can condemn the people who live in that area. By doing this, you can make people so dissatisfied and disillusioned that they will sooner or later express an urgent desire to leave the area (and, in doing so, make it available for people who want to take it over).

That was in the late 1960s. Over the past 50 years, what has the city done? It "stood pat," "held its hand," "watched and exercised patience" while the area slowly deteriorated to the state where it is now. You cannot blame the black community for North Omaha's condition; these are residents who have survived *despite* the presence of the city and state.

Now, for that "art center" that the article mentions.

In a recently released report out of the Chicago Cultural Policy Center, *Set in Stone: Building America's New Generation of Arts Facilities, 1994-2008,* the point made was whether or not "new homes for the arts institutions are worth the billions lavished on them" (Wilonsky, 2012: p. 1-E). This point is only relevant in that there are some people out there who are concerned about such contributions to the arts and whether or not the structures are worth it.

This may not be relevant here. No person is spending millions, let alone billions on an art facility in any black community. These are reserved, as I've witnessed, for downtown areas so that they can attract what I call "the white arts:" the opera, the symphony and the ballet. The tiny art center that is planned for North Omaha – even the name is grandiose and inappropriate – does not fall into this category. But the fact must be made that in major cities where these facilities are being built, there are questions asked regarding the sensibility of the monies being spent.

Now here's where the general topic becomes relevant: the function of art.

As an artist, I have always subscribed to the belief that there is no "art for art's sake," that are has a message. Black people's art is art that expresses a way of life and a value system; you find few of us painting oranges in a bowl or birds singing in trees. This is the basis of only one part of my concern: the second is that art is, for the most part, a leisure activity.

Who, in North Omaha, is going to have time to tour an arts facility? Who is going to have time to stand around while a visiting artist explains his or her work? The work of Magdalena Thompson in South Omaha shows what I mean: when she opened up El Museo Latina, she had it rough the first few years, and most of her patrons then, as now, are white folks, not Latinos. In North Omaha, as stigmatized as it is, how dare the city put an "arts center" less than a half a mile from a museum that they've ignored and another arts facility that they never really supported in the first place?

But when it comes to North Omaha, what is being done doesn't have to make any long-term sense, as long as it quells the "we want something" now childish impetuousity of black people in the area; a people who have been so starved for acceptance that they have often doubted their own humanity. An arts center?

The article continues, and even with one of the World Herald's best reporters, Cindy Gonzalez, attempting to overlook or underplay the issue of "race," it still comes through loud and clear.

> Anchoring the project is the old Fair Deal Cafe, referred to fondly as the "Black City Hall" because of its reputation as the gathering place years ago for north Omaha leaders, deal-makers and visiting politicians. The cafe on 2118 N. 24th St., which shut its doors years ago, and the nearby St. Martin de Porres Center are to be restored as an art gallery and workshop for youth and artists (Gonzalez, 2012).

Only in North Omaha would a café serve as an "anchor" to a community development project. Maybe in a small shopping mall or an area like the old Market, which is retail-oriented, but not a cultural haven like North Omaha. This is an area that was about more than "stop and shop;" it was an area that was, first of all, a place where you could engage with other human beings on what was going on in the world. All up and down the street black people passes and greeted one another, oftentimes kids in tow. These white people and their "developer" sidekicks, are working to redefine North Omaha in their own image and interests.

Those interests are market oriented and revenue driven. *They could care less about black culture because they've shown no care or concern for black people!*

This is not the first time that "artsy bullshit" or what I call the "Vincent Van Go and Get'em" approach has been used in the name of black "community development." The ministers, in all their wisdom, got behind a project for a postage stamp sized park dedicated to Martin Luther King, Jr., along the northwest corner of 24th and Lake. The city came up with a Preston Love Arts and Humanities Museum (part of the title stolen from one of my proposals) and didn't as Preston anything about it (I was on the phone with him when they announced it). The Museum had no collectibles, was lacking in clientele and is now nothing more than a rental space.

Another time they thought that a small park with an expensive statue was a nice statue. A statue of a jazz man blowing his instrument with some woman watching on. This same "plan" included colorful bricks to adorn the sidewalk. This is what they call "development" when it comes to the people whose poverty generated the grant money in the first place.

If there was respect for the area, locals would be contacted and consulted regarding historical figures, activities and structures that could be honored by naming parts of the area after them. If the Fair Deal was called the "Black City Hall" – and it was called that – then where are references to the leadership, backwards though most of it was. Where is the reference to the 4CL, the Mothers for Adequate Welfare, the Ideal Improvement Club, the Eure Family, or individuals like Sara Rountree, Charlotte Shropshire, Lerlean Johnson, Lawrence McVoy, Buddy Hogan, and so on?

You can write generically about a "gathering place years ago for north Omaha leaders, deal-makers and visiting politicians," but even when you break down this vanilla-and-oat-meal statement, you can see racism – that is, once you know the history.

Why did they gather? Who were they discussing? What were the conditions under which many of these gatherings took place? As for the "deal-makers," who were they, and what kind of deals could have possibly been made with North Omaha being in the condition that it is in today? We know the answer: selfish and short-term deals, of course! Bribes, kickbacks, co-optation and the rest of the tricks that take place when white people want to "colonize" an area: get people who look like the ones you want to control and pay them to be your eyes and ears (translation: snitch). Then they give it a fancy name like "liaison" or they create an organization with a name the people will respect, like "North Omaha Community Development" or "North Omaha Rebuilding Committee" or "Project Renaissance."

And who were the "visiting politicians"? Were they from Russia, Africa or the Middle East? Of course not. Since Omaha has always been residentially and racially segregated, the "visitors" were from none other than the city administration, the county and the state, who were going on "safari" by visiting the black community or, as they used to call it, "the slums." These "visiting politicians" visited for what? Where are the fruits of their labor, legislation and plans for North Omaha? What has gotten better since 1977 as a result of those "visits"? You can see for yourself.

Not a damn thing.

Those visits were in line with the "deal-makers" statement made earlier. These people white men coming to North Omaha, cutting deals, and then skidaddling out of the area back to suburbia. They surely weren't hear to stick around for any length of time, to take a tour of the area, to meet with any local activists who might deserve to have their say on what was going on. No, it was the same black people who consider themselves "deal makers" but are actually treated like the "favorite sons" of the city, given bullshit organization titles, get their palms greased and then, through trial-and-error, who on "development projects" that would be considered a joke in any other city of considerable size.

These developers include the St. Martin de Porres Center, known more for handing out food baskets now, but it is named after a man who dedicated his life to the uplift of North Omaha. So take that great name, take a building that was at one time a citadel of black planning, and turn them as white as snow with some irrelevant "re-design" of an area that has the future of white people coming back in mind. This is not about appeasing black people or doing something for self-esteem of the natives: it is all about the riverfront, proximity to it, taking back the city's flat land, and building inducements for white yuppies to come back to the central city, right near downtown where their jobs are, and have a good time. Even Warren Buffett has his nose stuck in the project, or so I've heard.

When you really don't care about a project, you put people in charge of it who you can appease. That way, if it fails, who cares? If it doesn't then that person can add it to their community development resume. Take note, then, of the following:

> Funds for that $280,000 piece, are still being raised, said
> Annette Artherton of the Omaha Economic Development
> Corporation, which is heading the district revival.
> Artherton said funds have been secured for the housing
> portion about a block away along both sides of 25th Street.
> Those dollars will come from a combination of federal, state
> and city funds and Wells Fargo bank. (Gonzalez, 2012).

Still being raised? Funds have been secured? This kind of nitpicking, parcel-by-parcel approach to development flies in the face of the process under which it is supposed to be done. First, you hire a developer and designer. Then, you get the design. Third, then with these in hand, you the money for the project. It is only after these things have been done that you notify the media about the coming of a project to an area that has been long neglected. By doing it there way there is room for on going stall tactics, errors and when it comes the residents, more disappointment.

The key words are right there: "still being raised," "district revival," "housing portion." That housing portion is the CDBG money that black poverty generated. The dollars from those banks are LOANS that will have to be paid back because, you see: an important element is missing from all this "praise-Jesus!-de-white-man-is-gonna-fix-up-de-ghetto! Rhetoric and promises: everything involved is generating money for the outside white interests that are involved.

It is called a "commercial corridor" for a reason. The question is: who is going to own and control the commercial sites? The apartment housing for seniors is no gift: it will be rented, probably through HUD, and the bank will have to be repaid somehow. The single homes for families? No gift. They will be sold and someone will pocket a hefty profit because the locations will be near downtown, near the riverfront, and close to Creighton University (which has done its share of land-grabbing over the years). An arts center? For what? They have the Great Plains Black Museum and the Preston Love Arts and Humanities "museum" which are already empty and in need of attention.

Here is another subtle area where the variable of racism is key: white people have conceded that black people dominate the arts, just as we dominate sports. But they will only concede certain arts: visual, poetry, drama. They still want to impose the opera, the ballet and the symphony on the world, which is why all major cities provide optimum support for these three areas. But when you're talking about an "arts center" in North Omaha, you're talking about a building that will have rooms for leasing and in a word, generate revenue for someone: this is all part of the plan, and I've written this elsewhere. The only time the city is going to do something for black people is if the money to do it with is free and there is some type of profit or revenue generation that benefits THEM (white folks). The history of this city's relationship with North Omaha clearly bears this out.

Those of us who have been involved in the race struggle in Omaha have seen and heard all this before. As you read the following paragraph, remember that this article is a fluff piece for a project that is not even underway and that it is filled with the same vague code words which show that "doubt," more than ditch-digging, is fundamental to this project's success:

> More than 50 neighborhood and business leaders watched
> Friday as city leaders turned the first shovels of dirt on the 40-

unit apartment building for people 55 and older. Across the street, construction work has begun for the five single family homes. "This is a big day for north Omaha," said Willie Barney of the Empowerment Network. He and others said the construction should help spur continued economic and social development of north Omaha. (Gonzalez, 2012).

Take note that "neighborhood and business leaders" are separated by title. But this is also a separation based on the former being more about influence while the latter is more about power. Why couldn't they otherwise be "neighborhood business leaders"? The answer is clear: in that neighborhood (North Omaha) all of the business is controlled by outsiders who, in turn, leave the neighborhood level decisions to black people. Subtly, neighborhood leader means blacks and business leader means white. In addition to the residential and racial segregation that I earlier charged, Omaha is also economically segregated; where that not the case, "black leaders," "neighborhood leaders" and even the term "North Omaha" would not be necessary to describe the racism that permeates the city. But each one carries a label and buzzword that those involved in community, city and social planning are well aware of.

Five single family homes? Only in north Omaha would the construction of five homes be major news. And then they get Willie Barney to say, "This is a big day for North Omaha." These words have been uttered scores of times in the past, and what happens? That "big day" either never arrives, is never fulfilled if it does arrive and even when fulfilled, some outside interest profits from it. The Kellom Mall was supposed to be a "big deal," the Kellom Apartments were supposed to be a "big deal," as were the renovated Garden Apartments. The construction of the Family Housing building on 24th and Lake was supposed to be a "big deal" as was the renovation of the Blue Lion Center and before that, the old Safeway building and its transformation into the Omaha Small Business Network, which has done literally nothing toward inspiring relevant new businesses in the area.

What about the other "big deals": the introduction of North Omaha Community Development, the arrival of George Garnett from "Yale" with a degree in political science? All gone bust. Where were these "neighborhood leaders" when all this was taking place? Nowhere to be found because, in one form or another, they're all beholden to or tied to the system itself. And as we know, *"the hand that feeds, controls."*

Barney of the self-proclaimed "Empowerment Network," makes a statement that again, raises more doubt. He states that, "the construction should help spur continued economic and social development of north Omaha." The key word in this claim is "should." Where is the certainty? Where are the guarantees? If what they're doing is so well planned out, where are the assurances? The best they can say is that what's taking place SHOULD spur continued economic and social development?

What if I was building a freeway and I said, "this *should* help people get from one area to another." Wouldn't that raise doubts? How about if I was an airplane pilot and before takeoff I said, "This plane *should* have us there in two or three hours?" What if you were on the operating table about to have heart surgery, I was your doctor and I told you, "this operation *should* go according to procedure?"

If every scenario just presented you would have doubts and begin second-guessing about the qualifications of the person, the project and the general intentions of people that would spend a lot of money, make promises and then come up with the word should as a quasi-guarantee. What are they doing? They are hedging their bets, they are covering their collective asses because if they provide a guarantee, they could be held liable. And when it comes to North Omaha and its deterioration, it's always about pointing the finger at the residents themselves, or at the riots of the 1960s or at some other entity than at where responsibility squarely goes: on decisions made by the City of Omaha Planning Department.

One last point where Barney says that the construction should help "spur continued economic and social development of north Omaha." Social development? For whom and for what? If you spur economic development, social development is a given; so why is it necessary to distinguish between the two. I'll tell you why: the "social planning" that Omaha is involved in is inextricably bound to a "relocation strategy." As part of "helping North Omaha," the goal of the city is to change (alter) the boundaries by moving black people further to the Northwest, away from downtown, away from the riverfront and away from the leisure and frolic that is being planned for those whites who will be returning to the area in the name of "reinvestment." This then, is the focus and fulcrum of any "social planning" that the city of Omaha has now, has always had, and will continue to have.

The article concludes:

> The Fair Deal Urban District marks the beginning of the
> broader, $1.43 billion North Omaha Village Revitalization
> Plan, which was announced in the summer of 2011 and is to
> be completed in phases and funded by a combination of public
> and private funds. (Gonzalez, 2012).

Who named this the "North Omaha Village Revitalization Plan"? It had to have been one of those self-appointed negro leaders who still thinks that the adage, "It takes a village to raise a child" is something novel. Let's look at the name of this "plan," because people in these power positions know the function of a name and the power that a name carries and what it projects, not only to the locals but the people from other parts of the region who might be hearing about it. Let's look at it logically.

To begin with, you cannot revitalize something that never existed. There never was a "village" because a village, like an ideal community, is self-contained and has certain characteristics. The residents of North Omah are consumers, and that is where they enter the economy: they eat and consume that has already been planted, developed and grown in the primary and secondary component of the economy. North Omahans join in at the tertiary sector. This is no village: it is a dependent enclave that has been systematically neglected for centuries and used only when Federal grant dollars or white interests are involved. It's not about the morals of the issue; it's about what the market can bear. There is no village anywhere except in the minds of people who want to pretend that they care about Africa, but who don't give a damn about the Africans in America.

Secondly, how much "broader" is this village revitalization plan going to be? How much of North Omaha will these city planners, their development-related cronies, and their negro lackeys carve out for themselves? Third, why does it have to be completed in phases? If they have the macrolevel idea and plan (the village), and then are working on a single component of it, why don't they just work on all of the components simultaneously? I'll tell you why: because they don't have the money to do it all at one time, and better to hunker down and do part of it and leave the rest hanging (like they did the North Omaha freeway at one point) than to stand pat and not do anything at all, lest the 'natives' get restless.

They plan and dissect and divide and the only people included in all this are those in their inner circle. So-called "black leaders" are allowed in and may or not get paid to keep the word to themselves. Not even the normally trustworthy ministers and preachers are allowed into these meetings, because these meetings involve power, and that is one thing whites in Omaha are not going to allow to any black person: *influence* is one thing, *power* is quite another.

CONCLUSION

This paper has been a response to yet another "announcement" regarding "attempts" to "help North Omaha." As stated, North Omaha's part in this scenario is that North Omaha is in the perfect geographical position to expand on white leisure activity. An area that has long time been the segregated bane of the white establishment, North Omaha is nevertheless the area with the best flat land, the nicest avenues and boulevards, optimum proximity to the Missouri River and minutes away from downtown, where there are more than 25,000 jobs.

This paper has endeavored to explain the reasons for the "Fair Deal Urban District," reasoning that goes much deeper than professed claims of "wanting to help the area." This paper also charges that there exists, "placation and long-term takeover strategies," and documents decades of various "plans" and "programs" that were used as a smokescreen to slowly encroach on the black community. The paper focuses also on the role that the major newspaper, The Omaha World Herald, has played in aiding and abetting the city in these plans. This "help" includes outright lies, unsubstantiated "projects" of more jobs and improvement, quotes from individuals who offer no evidence, and the selective interviewing of the people involved in the "plans" with no evidence of their qualifications or commitment to the area.

Again, had the city of Omaha properly spent the more than $200 million that it has received since 1975 on the North Omaha area, there would already be a thriving area where the ghetto is now located. Furthermore, how can we expect the city to spend almost a *billion and a half dollars* on North Omaha when they wouldn't do the right thing with the $200 plus *million* that they already had?

The project shouldn't be called "FAIR Deal Urban District," but instead, "FARE Deal Urban District. We know, for example, that the word "fare" is defined as, "the price of conveyance or passage in a bus, train, airplane, or other vehicle." It can also refer to, "a person or persons who pay to be conveyed in a vehicle, paying passenger." It can be "a person who hires a public vehicle and tis driver."

All of these involve a payment to "ride," as it were. Black people in North Omaha have been overcharged for almost everything, from utilities and cable television to their telephone landlines, the rent they pay and even the food that they purchase. They are, indeed, fares in the sense that they have paid and, for at least a century, they have figuratively been "taken on a ride." This proposed project is another one and it appears that the Empowerment Network as white power brokers (elites) convinced that all of North Omaha is "on board."

Don't be so sure.

WHAT MIGHT HAVE BEEN: THE PORTLAND, ORE., EXAMPLE

Never take what you can't replace or improve, the old saying teaches. I have well documented the scams and chicanery that mayors and city planners have run on the cities of America in their on-going abuses of Community Development Block Grant funding. Omaha is hardly an exception and, at least in my case, I would consider it the prototype, having gotten away with so much fraud, false applications and outright lies for over three decades.

The following 2007 article, "Working to free residents from poverty's grip, the author paints a picture that other cities might want to emulate. This situation will be addressed showing what Omaha might do and with my proposals being offered up as solutions.

> THESIS: As Portland continues to transform the way it does business, there are many cities nationwide that can learn from their experiences (Knox, 2007)

The fact is, one middle sized city out of more than 1,200 who receive CDBG funding is a statement in and of itself. Why aren't the cities that do all the bragging and have all the populations – Dallas, New York, Los Angeles, Chicago, Detroit, Philadelphia, to name a few – why aren't they trying to engage in innovative strategies that would leave lasting and long-term, positive impacts on their inner cities?

The solution was simple enough, as explained below:

> In 2004, Portland, took a bold step to reduce poverty in its urban neighborhoods. After years of funding community-based organizations to help a lot of people a little bit, the city's Bureau of Housing and Community Development (BHCD) believed it could be more effective by pursuing a focused strategy founded on best practices. (Knox, 2007)

To begin with, don't speed read through the previous paragraph but instead, try to engage in critical thinking as you see the words. I have a question: why would you "reduce poverty in an urban neighborhood" unless you planned on keeping the people there? Why not eliminate poverty, period?! Why just target the poor areas because there are surely poor people in middle class neighborhoods as well. And why merely "reduce" poverty? What is the formula? What percentage or level of poverty is acceptable or safe? When white folks talk about reductions, what they really mean is working toward making something "manageable" which further translates to mean manageable by THEM!

What are these "best practices"? In the past I've raised questions about the lack of cultural competency and inter-racial input in such practices. These practices are usually ethnocentric in their basis and corporate oriented in their implementation. Because of this, a statements comes to mind: "you can't teach what you don't know, and you can't lead where you won't go."

But the plan, in the case of Portland, sounds logical. Check it out:

> From that belief, Portland launched its Economic Opportunity Initiative in 2004, focusing community development block

> grant (CDBG) funds on increasing the income of low-income
> individuals and families. The initiative is a citywide
> poverty reduction program with a goal of increasing the
> incomes and assets of low-income residents by a minimum of
> 25 percent within three years. Two factors led BHCD to
> transition from revitalization to income generation as a
> poverty-reduction strategy— changes in the community and in
> the city's strategic planning process (Knox, 2007)

Sounds great. But if you've studied history and race relations, you know that something that sounds like it is going to be focused in helping the poor is going to somehow end up benefitting more white folks, stabilizing the same system that created the problem in the first place, and in the end channel those poor on taking that money that they earn and using it to increase tax payments while doing away with traditional social services. Since the "new ideas" never stay around, those who have been helped usually end up being ousted from these programs when these programs fall short.

So let us take note of the following:

> Focus on those most in need: concentrate resources for real
> impact rather than spreading the money too thinly. Move from
> a geographic to a population focus, and shift the focus from
> those below 80 percent of the median family income to those
> at or below 50 percent. Concentrate on three initiatives:
> workforce development for adults; a workforce development
> program for youth; and microenterprise or entrepreneurship
> projects that help participants start or expand small
> businesses.(Knox, 2007)

Let me go through this "plan" point by point and show that a program or project can sound logical or appear to be logical on paper, but when the variable of race is added, and then poverty is sprinkled in, the plan begins to appear as it really is: the will and right of those in power raised by free grant money to the level of sacred observance.

To begin with, the concentration of resources for "real impact." Real impact on who? Do they mean real impact on the community that is being focused on, or real impact on the media and outsiders who read about this "great program"? The latter is what usually takes place, or don't you remember earlier when I earlier cited an article from the Omaha World Herald from 1981 where the headline read, "North Omaha Sky Brightens." No such brightening took place and the "program" that was being written about was an abysmal failure. "Real impact" was an illusion, but it sounded good to those outside of the black community who were worried about "restless negroes."

In the case of Omaha, the restless negroes part is not a problem because most of them have been whipped into compliance after being fed one broken promise after another. These scams continue in the guise of new buildings going up as whites chase grants. They expand a facility to deal with black girls when its found that the teen pregnancy rate is high – that means more grant money. They build a structure called "North Pointe, supposedly for black boys after it is revealed that Omaha is number one in black child poverty and the black on black youth homicide rate is tops in the nation for a city this size.

As they chase the grant money and make sure that whites are in charge of these "programs," they hook up with a local corporation or a millionaire to ensure short-term funding. They hire a grantwriter who can bring in long-term funding. By constructing and expanding buildings ("bricks and mortar projects") they give white developers jobs and reserve the land that the structure is on, for future possible use. They take up the space so black people won't get their hands on it.

So to talk of "real impact" should raise the question, "real impact for whom and for what"? I think that this paper has made it clear that those with the decision making power are not about to disperse their concentrated "pocket of poverty," which is the key to continuing to receive future funding.

Secondly, the move from a "geographic focus to a population focus." When it comes to low income people and minorities, in most instance the geography and population are both compartmentalized, meaning that there is high density and a lot of people are crowded into a small section of the "geography." This is what constitutes what the government calls a "pocket of poverty" and is one of the four elements that qualifies cities like Portland for the Community Development Block Grant.

If, for instance, during the "population focus" you say "north side" or "black people," since most black people are concentrated on the north side, this is the same as the "geographic focus." In Omaha, if you say North Omaha, anyone who knows the city knows that this is the "geographic area" that is predominantly black. If you say the "north side" in Milwaukee, it's black; if you say the south side, its white. The west side of Chicago is black, and the north side of Minneapolis is also predominantly African-American. These are FACTs based on both population and geography.

Third, shifting the focus from those below 80 percent of the median family income to those at or below 50 percent. It sounds like a good idea because the latter group are the ones who are the most poor. But what are you going to do? They are the most poor because they are the most segregated and isolated. They are the most segregated and isolated because of the lack of jobs or finances. Most of them lack that because they are not qualified for many jobs or haven't got the education. So what sounds like benevolence is really just another way to get more people who are more desperate, most impoverished and most in need to become a part of the PROGRAMS that the white man controls: programs aimed at training, job development, getting your General Education Diploma (GED), attending Adult Basic Education (ABE) courses, dress for success, resume development and so on. So on one end you appear to be helping the poor, but in reality, you're helping yourself TO the poor.

Fourth, the first of the three proposed "initiatives" – a workforce development program for adults. That's been tried and it doesn't seem to be working. You're training adults for jobs, but who is going to provide the jobs. These people had to return to a training program and haven't been in school for years because they thought the job that they had would last forever. Even now, I'm writing the essays and term papers for older people who are trying to "return to school" for some "additional education." The training might work but it's a long process; and once "trained," you head out to the work place to apply for jobs and compete with much younger people. Workforce development should develop the workforce psychologically and technically in order to prepare for the "baby boomer employee," the ones who had jobs but lost them due to decisions that their employers made. That's an entirely different mindset.

Fifth, a workforce development program for youth. By youth they really mean young adults and then you have a more complicated situation. The workplace will hire them part time and after school, but when it comes to full time, they have to be adult-age to even land a job. And then when they do they are going to be paid less than the "adults" who do the same job. In the age of downsizing and early retirement, when these jobs bring kids on they pay them a fraction of what the previous "adult" employee was making. As is the case with most of these ideas, the system benefits and profits from the projects and programs created by the CDBG. The poor receive training and crumbs, but the system gets the big paying jobs, the job titles, the status and the credit.

Sixth and finally, the third initiative, which is the creation of a microenterprise or entrepreneurship projects to start or expand small businesses. Many cities are violating the principles of entrepreneurship projects because they offer LOANS to those who have bad credit. If not that, then the business incubators that are supposed to provide low cost office space for start up businesses are keeping these businesses far too long. In Omaha, for example, their Omaha Startup Business Network (OSBN) has offices filled with wannabe business people. They pay a small rent, but they are supposed to only be there a short time and they are supposed to be getting trained.

But in Omaha, there are people in that building – a supposed minority business development building -- who have been there, paying rent, for two decades! The training they receive is questionable and even the resources that are supposed to be provided – access to copy machines, access to the computer room and so on – show that these business people are being treated like children. For instance, the computer room is open from 9 to 5, but closed over the lunch break. And it's not even open on weekends. Meanwhile the rents are used to maintain the building. But the source of the program is the free money offered through Community Development Block Grants that, in turn, come to Omaha based on black poverty. And the building, located in the heart of the black community, is doing little or nothing to assist minority businesses.

Furthermore,

> Other economic development efforts had a trickle-down approach for years (tax incentives, physical revitalization, tax reform, regional assistance to lure companies), and it hadn't worked for low-income residents. BHCD made the decision to change to a bottom-up approach.(Knox, 2007)

The words of Knox betray him. Look at how he phrases his point. He says that other development "efforts" had a trickle-down approach. The reason why they failed is contained in his explanation: they were "efforts." When the white man knows he's not going to succeed, he talks in retrospect about his vaunted "efforts." They are not successes – they are "efforts." They "try" to help the negroes, but usually fall short. Trickle down, one of Reagan's bullshit strategies, was not designed to work. How could it when, on the way "down," any idea or initiative is going to be screened by those at the middle, peeled off, nibbled on and gouged so that by the time it gets to the bottom, there's nothing left! That's why the successful Japanese system of "bottoms up authority" – also known as the "Ringi system" – has propelled them to the top of industry and education!

And now for these high falutin' "best practices:"

> BHCD identified best practices from smaller projects throughout the country and implemented them on a citywide scale. Now it invests in a coordinated portfolio of more than 30 projects incorporating these best practices as a foundation: (Knox, 2007)

Best practices devoid of cultural sensitivity, cultural competence and a diversity focus are nothing more than corporate practices being pawned off as being universally applicable. The white man's arrogance knows no bounds; how can they be "best practices" when they've only been proven effective for white organizations or for black managed organizations that are nevertheless controlled (through funding and seats on the board of directors) by whites? It's akin to referring to the color of stockings and bras and panties as being "nude," even though the colors are designed for the white woman's pinkish white skin. What about black women? What about brown women? What about Asian women? The color "nude" becomes universally accepted, just like "best practices" because the designers and decision makers have the power of definition; they TELL people of color what is right or wrong, or which way is up or down, and we fall for the okey-doke.

Therefore, what Knox defines in the following paragraph has already existed:

> Projects serve groups of people united by some common characteristic such as ethnicity, race or entrepreneurial ambition. For example, a project for immigrant Eastern European metal workers builds on their technical experience and trains them to use American equipment. (Knox, 2007)

Again, if white folks write or talk long enough, they eventually fall into or expose their own racist traps. For instance, the preceding excerpt says that, "Projects serve groups of people united by some common characteristic such as ethnicity, race or entrepreneurial ambition." But in reality all of these variables are related, because of the purpose of CDBG, by class: all are low income, all are impoverished and most are segregated.

Secondly, were the city and this nation not racially segregated, the one variable that would be "common" would be that all are "Americans." Remember that myth? So when race and ethnicity are somehow profitable, programs can be developed to address the fact that race and ethnicity are grounds for being isolated and/or ignored by the city. The solution? To create programs to assuage white conscience while addressing the needs of these racial and ethnic groups (under white guidance, of course) and creating programs that provide jobs for the white social worker, intake officer, home visitor, classroom trainer, program service director and so on. Getting rich while feigning a moral concern.

Third, take note of the example that they use when it comes to ethnicity. They cite as an example, " a project for immigrant Eastern European metal workers builds on their technical experience and trains them to use American equipment." These "eastern Europeans," in many cases, are dark brown people who think they're white. They come over here, in many cases, with advanced degrees and get to stay because there are special visas that this country offers for talented immigrants. So they have money back where they came from. Now they can draw on that and also quality for special programs just because they're immigrants.

To be an "immigrant" means you CHOSE to come over here, and you had the wherewithal to do so. When you get here you can afford to live wherever you choose to, and you're not treated with the kind of stigmatizing and degrading programs and approaches that the American born Blacks and Latinos are. And since most immigrants are white and Latino, these programs don't do much for African Americans, the only racial group subjected to 400-plus years of enslavement and continue to be the object of America's ire.

Knox further writes that,

> Projects provide extensive multifaceted support. Standard components include peer support and help with a range of issues, such as child care, tuition and transportation. Real change takes time. The initiative works with participants for three years to find a permanent way out of poverty. (Knox, 2007)

See? Note that, "the initiative works with participants for three years to find a permanent way out of poverty." Hasn't the current situation with the anticipated cutbacks in CDBG taught these white men that there is nothing "permanent" about any aspect of living in America? The only thing that might be permanent is the fact that there is nothing permanent! But by projecting "three years," you can guarantee yourself that many years of funding – a nice collection of paychecks for poverty pimps who, up front, guarantee that "poverty will end." This is bullshit.

You can't predict what the economy is going to do, how the world is going to react to America's greed and gluttony and so on. To project that there is a permanent way out of poverty is to admit that for all these decades, America has been full of shit with its various "approaches," "experiments," "programs," "projects," "training programs" and so on.

So this talk about providing "extensive and multifaceted supports" and all that – just more bullshit. The previous statement was written in 2007. I'll bet you a million dollars that if you go into Portland right now in 2014 – seven years after the fact – all that talk and promising won't be taking place. The programs will have failed and poverty will be as high, if not higher, than it was in 2007 when Knox wrote the previous article about this "initiative."

No matter what is pledged or promised, the end result is going to be the white man on top and people of color covering the rear. It's going to be the white man "managing" poverty while people of color and low-income whites make up the majority of the homeless and the hungry. Look at history and, in particular, look at the history of these Federal programs. The rhetoric sounds the same and the promises of "bright skies" are fed to the masses of people thanks to a cooperative, story-hungry media whose reporters and editors have mortgages and car notes to pay.

The article concludes, thusly:

> Portland moved swiftly to change the way scarce financial
> resources were invested in the city's people. By creating a
> pool of federal, regional and local funds, including matching
> grants from the United Way, BHCD provides financial
> resources to organizations trying to expand successful projects
> that reduce poverty (Knox, 2007).

Portland got scared. Just like a single parent that is going to go out and find some new sources of income (including tricks) if he or she thinks that the future looks grim in terms of income, Portland did the same thing. But with all the programs, projects and re-negotiating of the activities involved in the anti-poverty movement, note one thing remains constant: the hierarchy. The white man remains at the top, not matter what. That is the one constant that poverty programs can guarantee.

The article about Portland and its approach to using Community Development Block Grant funding was titled, "Working to Free Residents From Poverty's Grip." This is a mis-representation of what these planners and mayors are really doing. Omaha could benefit from the overall skeletal plan of what Portland ATTEMPTED to do, but you have to read between the lines and when you do that you can see how illogical and foolhardy it would be to try to end poverty without hurting white folks. That's who's in charge of those kinds of programs and that's why they were created. If you eliminated all of the poverty programs in a given city, the white unemployment rate would skyrocket. That's why they – and their negro lackeys – are known on the streets as "poverty pimps."

CONCLUSION

The destruction of black civilization began with white intervention into and its cultural insinuations upon the African continent centuries ago. As a result of that invasion, today's black community exists in segregated enclaves known as ghettos. Because of an event known as slavery, those blacks are the progeny of those who were, at one time, OWNED by white people. There has been no serious program since the "end of slavery" where the relationship between the owner (whites) and the owned (blacks) has changed all that much. Even all-black businesses that are located in all-black areas depend on white outside sources to survive.

The CDBG grant program is no exception. But what must be remembered is that it came into being as a result of black violence and threats of violence. White historians and educators have worked to give credit to the civil rights movement and are even trying to make it look like that movement was dominated by white folks. But in my view, as a Black scholar with the degrees to prove it, I credit the Black Power movement and the violence and the riots. White people respond when black people get angry. They (whites) have learned to laugh at ministers over the dinner table and scoff at that group that refers to itself as "civil rights leadership."

But violence – that's something they understand. And that explains the militarization of the local police forces, the upgrading of the National Guard, the existence of "urban assault" vehicles and all these movies about zombies and aliens attacking the "innocent" white race: they are merely transposing onto those creatures the way they envision a black threat. White people know what they would do if a racial group had enslaved THEIR race for 400 years – so they have always prepared. Their fear of an attack from Islam and other brown people shows that this fear still exists today in 2014.

North Omaha is being relocated and the whites who ran in the face of black violence during the 1960s want to return to an area that is close to the riverfront and close to downtown. The dearth of black leadership makes it easy for white interlopers to come into the community in the guise of "developers" since the blacks who claim to be developers don't know their asses from a hole in the ground. They can't do the work and when they do they want to do it half-assed. And those who can do the work have a racist inspector who is watching over them and finding any reason to tell them that their work is "unsatisfactory" and that they have to "start all over again." They do this as they hold onto their paychecks, further impairing the black contractors future job chances.

Those in charge of development have enlisted the assistance of sell-out negro leaders who will say and do what it takes to curry favor with the black ministers who, in turn, will do whatever it takes to pad their pockets and the collection plate. By combining sell out leadership with ill-prepared developers and ass backwards strategies, the white man can come in, complete with the "Missionary syndrome" that he has always had, and while standing in the middle of these goons, show them how inept they are based upon their own ill-preparedness, poor writing skills, lousy plans and comedic leadership.

The destruction of black civilization has taken place over a number of centuries but is now culminating in the white takeover of black communities all over the nation, much of it made possible with the help of poorly supervised and monitored Community Development Block Grants. The local cities are impeding black progress which has a cumulative effect because these "takeovers" are shared from city to city (like the Portland Plan) and black communities all over are being dispersed and/or relocated.

REFERENCES

Adams, John S. "A Geographical Basis for Urban Public Policy. **Professional Geographer.** Vol. 31. No. 2. May.

Aiello, John and A. Baum (eds.) **Residential Crowding and Design.** New York: Plenum Press. 1979.

Applied Real Estate Analysis, Inc. **Draft--New Retail Development Potential, 30th and Ames, Omaha, Nebraska: Prepared for City of Omaha and North Omaha Community.** Chicago, IL: Real Estate and Policy Planning Corporation. May 28, 1993.

Arnott, Richard J. and Frank D. Lewis. "The Transition of Land to Urban Use." **Journal of Political Economy**. Vol. 87. No. 1. February 1979.

Bach, Victor. "The New Federalism in Community Development." **Social Policy**. Vol. 7. No. 4. January-February 1977.

Bates, Timothy and Alfred E. Osborne, Jr. "The Reverse Effects of SBA Loans to Minority Wholesalers." **Urban Affairs Quarterly**. Vol. 15. no. 1. September 1979.

Beeder, David C. "Project Marks Anniversary: Line Forms at Kellom Knolls Apartments." **Omaha World Herald.** June 29, 1984.

Benson-Walker, Gwen. "In Retaliation: A Return to Tradition." **Essence.** July 1981.

Bish, Robert L. "Public Choice Theory for Comparative Research on Urban Service Delivery." **Comparative Urban Research**. Vol. 7. No. 1. 1979.

Boulay, Harvey. "Social Control Theories of Urban Politics." **Social Science Quarterly**. Vol. 59. No. 4. March 1979.

Bratt, Rachel. "The Neighborhood Movement: A Blip on the Landscape or a Blueprint for Action?" **Community Development Journal.** Vol. 20. No. 2. April 1985.

Brennan, M.A., Barnett, R., and Lesmeister, M. 2007. "Enhancing Leadership, Local Capacity, and Youth Involvement in the Community Development Process: Findings from a Survey of Florida Youth." **Journal of the Community Development** *Society* . 38(4).

Brown, Carolyn M. "How to Fight Mortgage Discrimination ... and Win!" **Black Enterprise.** Vol. 23. No. 12. July 1993.

Carolina Peacemaker, The. "Minority Land Loss to be Addressed on UNC TV Tuesday." December 2-December 8, 1993.

Cary, Lorene. "Why It's Not Just Paranoia: An American History of 'Plans' for Blacks." **Newsweek**. April 6, 1992.

Catlin, Robert A. "An Analysis of the Community Development Block Grant Program in Nine Florida Cities, 1975-1979." **Urban and Social Change Review**. Vol. 14. No. 1. Winter 1981.

Center for Public Affairs Research. **Omaha Conditions Survey: 1990.** Omaha, NE.: College of Public Affairs and Community Service. 1990.

Chambers, Ernie. "Legislative Floor Debate on LR 214." (a transcribed document). February 11, 1982.

----------------------. "Chambers Responds to NOCDs Tyler." **Omaha World Herald**. January 20, 1982.

Chavis, Benjamin F. Jr., "June 23rd: 'African American Land Loss Day'." **The Milwaukee Courier.** (no day, no month) 1991.

Clark, Thomas A. **Blacks in the Suburbs: A National Perspective.** New Brunswick, NJ: Rutgers University Press. 1979.

Clay, Phillip L. "Managing the Urban Reinvestment Process." **Journal of Housing.** Vol. 36. No. 9. October 1979.

Cohen, Rick. "Neighborhood Planning and Political Capacity." **Urban Affairs Quarterly**. Vol. 14. No. 3. March 1979.

Collison, Kevin. "Change is Byword in the Downtown." **Omaha World Herald.** June 17, 1984.

Colliver, Andrew and Moshe Semyonov. "Suburban Change and Persistence." **American Sociological Review**. Vol. 44. No. 3. June 1979.

Cooper, M. (2011, December 21). "Cities face tough choices as U.S. slashes block grants program." **New York Times**.

Cordes, Henry J. (2010, February 21). Epidemic of poverty, violence. **Omaha World Herald.**

Damond, Marietta E., Nancy L. Breuer & Ann E. Pharr. "The Evaluation of Setting and a Culturally Specific HIV/AIDS Curriculum: HIV/AIDS Knowledge and Behavioral Intent of African American Adolescents." **Journal of Black Psychology.** Vol. 19. No. 2. May 1993.

Deloria, Vine Jr. **Custer Died For Your Sins.** Norman, OK: University of Oklahoma Press. 1988.

Dingerman, Dennis. "Redlining and Mortgage Lending in Sacramento." **Annals of the Association of American Geographers.** Vol. 69. No. 2. June 1979.

Dommel, Paul R. and Michael J. Rich. "The Rich Get Richer: The Attenuation of Targeting Effects of the Community Development Block Grant Program." **Urban Affairs Quarterly.** Vol. 22. No. 4. June 1987.

Dorr, Robert. "Builders: Omaha Can Handle Additional Shopping Centers." **Omaha World Herald.** February 8, 1981.

Engelen, Rodney E. "What is the Future for Downtown Retailing in Middle America? A Middle Market Malaise." **Urban Land**. Vol. 38. No. 9. October 1979.

Fierheller, John W. "Approaches to the Study of Urban Crime: A Review Article." **Urban History Review**. Vol. 8. No. 2. October 1979.

Flowerdew, Robin. "Spatial Patterns of Residential Segregation in a Southern City." **Journal of American Studies**. Vol. 13. No. 1. April 1979.

Foy, Nicole. "Workshop Tackles North Omaha Woes." **Omaha World Herald.** October 22, 1993. p. 15.

--------------. "Anchor Store Being Sought at 30th, Ames." **Omaha World Herald.** February 3, 1994. p. 13.

Frey, William H. "Black In-migration, White Flight and the Changing Economic Base of the Central City." **Institute for Research on Poverty. Discussion Papers, #540-79.**

---------------------. "Central City White Flight." **American Sociological Review.** Vol. 44. No. 3. June 1979.

Gentile, A. (2007, July). Senators request more funds for CDBG: Without increases, recipients may cut programs. **American City and County**, 122, (7).

Gilbert, L.F. Sr. (2011, February 19). Mayor's corner: CBBG funds are of tremendous importance to Lewiston. **Twin City Times**. Retrieved from http://www.twincitytimes.com/events/mayor%E2%80%99s-corner-cdbg-funds-are-of-tremendous-importance-to-lewiston

Gleiber, Dennis W. and Mary Ann Steger. "Decentralization, Local Politics and the Community Development Block Grant Program in Milwaukee." **Publius.** Vol. 13. No. 3. Summer 1983.

Goetze, Rolf. "Urban Neighborhoods in Transition." **Social Policy.** Vol. 10. No. 2. September/October 1979.

Goetz, Edward G. **Shelter Burden: Local Politics and Progressive Housing Policy**. Philadelphia, PA: Temple University Press. 1993.

Gonzalez, C. (2012, September 15). North Omaha's Old Fair Deal Cafe is center of $12.2 million plan. **The Omaha World Herald.**

Gonzalez, C. (Sept 15, 2012) "New 'Fair Deal Urban District' hailed as 'kick-start project' for North O". **The Omaha World Herald**

Gruen, Claude, Nina J. Gruen and Diane Spies. "Property Rights Ain't What They Used To Be: The Defense of Socially Worthy Projects." **Urban Land**. Vol. 39. No. 8. September 1979.

Gupta, Udayan. "Staking Your Ground in the Black Community." **Essence.** May 1980.

Hall, John Stuart. "Fitting the Community Development Block Grant Program to Local Politics: Who is the Tailor?" **Publius.** Vol. 13. No. 3. Summer 1983.

Hanlon, Gene. "Blacks Seek City Services." **Omaha World Herald.** September 27, 1980.

Hare, Nathan. "Black Ecology." **The Black Scholar.** Vol. 1. No. 6.   April 1970.

Harris, Hamil R. "Whatever Happened to Enterprise Zones?" **Black Enterprise.** April 1992.

Hesse-Biber, Sharlene. "The Ethnic Ghetto and Private Welfare: A Case Study of Southern Italian Immigrants to the United States, 1880-1914." **Urban Land and Social Change Review.** Vol. 12. No. 2. Summer 1979.

Holeywell, R. (2012, March). CDBG takes another hit. **Governing.**

Hord, Bill. "Coming to Nebraska This Year: Enterprise Zones." **Omaha World Herald.** January 2, 1994.

Iutcovich, Joyce Miller and Mark Iutcovich. "The Politics of Evaluation Research: A Case Study of Community Development Block Grant Funding for Human Services." **Evaluation and Program Planning.** Vol. 10. No. 1. 1987.

Johnson-Elie, Tannette. "Insurers Lose Round in Redline Case: Court Ruling Paves Way for Discrimination Suits." **Milwaukee Sentinel.** October 22, 1992.

Jones, Stacey. "Problems With Home Mortgage Practices Hit Home (Part 1). **Milwaukee Courier.** September 23, 1989.

------------------. "Problems With Home Mortgage Practices Hit Home (Part 2). **Milwaukee Courier.** September 30, 1989.

Jordon, Steve. "Closer Monitoring Sought for North Omaha Lending." **The Omaha World Herald**. October 31, 1994.

Kasarda, John D. and Morris Janowitz. "Community Attachment in Mass Society." **American Sociological Review.** Vol. 39. June 1974.

King, Larry. "City Services Compared--Analysis: Northeast Gets Hearty Share." **Omaha World Herald**. August 31, 1980.

----------------. "Shop, Offices Cornerstone: Remodeling Project to Anchor 24th, Lake." **Omaha World Herald**. September 16, 1981.

Knox, L. (2007, Summer). Portland, Ore. Working to free residents from poverty's grip. **Bridges.**

Kreisman, Richard. "Hard Winter Tough on Restaurant Chains." **Advertising Age.** February 15, 1982.

Lange, Jeffrey K. and David J. O'Brien. "Needs and Formulas: Operationalizing Justice in Community Development Funding." **Sociological Focus.** Vol. 11. No. 4. 1978.

Larson, Jan. "Density is Destiny." **American Demographics.** Vol. 15. No. 2. February 1993.

Liebschutz, Sarah F. "Neighborhood Conservation: Political Choices Under the Community Development Block Grant Program." **Publius.** Vol. 13. No. 3 Summer 1983.

Long, Norton. "The Local Community as an Ecology of Games." **American Journal of Sociology.** Vol. LXIV. November 1958.

Lovell, Catherine. "Community Development Block Grant: The Role of Federal Requirements." **Publius.** Vol. 13. No. 3. Summer 1983.

Lowry, Ira S. and Bruce W. Ferguson. **Development Regulation and Housing Affordability**. The Urban Land Institute. 1992.

Maier, Peter and David Machmias. "An Evaluation of Community Development Block Grant Decisionmaking: Executive Dominance vs. Issue Networks." **Journal of Policy Studies.** Vol. 18. No. 3. Spring 1990.

Malanga, S. (2010, Spring). Block grants forever: A deathless program and its long history of failure. **City Journal**, 20, (2).

Martin, Thad. "Harris Neck: Georgia Blacks Fight to Regain Ancestral Land." **Ebony.** July 1983.

Massey, Douglas S and Nancy A. Denton. "Suburbanization and Segregation in U.S. Metropolitan Areas." **American Journal of Sociology.** Vol. 94. No.3. November 1988.

Matters, Philip. "Hot Child in the City: Urban Crisis, Urban Renaissance and Urban Struggle." **Radical America.** Vol. 13. No. 5. September/October 1979.

McCoy, Frank. "Ending the Zone Wars." **Black Enterprise**. September 1992.

McKanna, C.V. Jr. (1994). Seeds of destruction: Homicide, race and justice in Omaha, 1880-1920. **Journal of American Ethnic History**, 14, (1). 65-90.

Morgan, David R. and Robert E. England. "Evaluating a Community Development Block Grant Program: A Citizen's Group Perspective." **Policy Studies Journal**. Vol. 13. No. 2. December 1983.

Morganthau, Tom and Marcus Mabey. "Losing Ground: New Fears and Suspicions as Black America's Outlook Grows Bleaker." **Newsweek**. April 6, 1992.

Morse, John B. **The Efforts of Omaha's Black Community to Overcome the Great Depression.** (A research paper submitted to Dr. William Pratt, History 532A. University of Nebraska at Omaha. December 1971.

Mulcahy, Colleen. "Minority Agents Look to Boost Inner-City Business." **National Underwriter**. Vol. 98. Issue 8. February 21, 1994.

Myers, Sibyl. "Promoter Sees North Omaha Changes: 'New Facelift' Could Become Noticeable Within 6 Months." **Omaha World Herald** (no date)

----------------. "North Omaha Rebuilding By 'Working Together'." **Omaha World Herald**. September 12, 1982.

Nelson, Andrew J., Gaardner, Nancy & Conley, Alia. (2017, June 6). Man who died after being tased by police was mentally ill, off his medication and lost in Omaha, his mother says. **Omaha World Herald.**

Nelson, Jill. "Black Dollars: Taking Control." **Essence.** September 1986

Norman, Jack. "Full Data Confirm Wider Race Gap." **The Milwaukee Journal.** November 5, 1992.

------------------. "Lenders Tackle Mortgage Gap: Large Banks, S&L Start Inquiries Into Why Racial Disparities Persist." **The Milwaukee Journal**. November 8, 1992.

North Omaha Community Development. **Response: 24th and Lake Street Development Plan.** Omaha, NE: NOCD. (no date)

Nover, Aimee R. "Social Policy in Relation to the Community Development Block Grant Process." **Social Thought.** Vol. 8. No. 1. 1982.

Olson, Chris. "Neighborhood Big Factor In Price of a Home." **Omaha World Herald**. December 19, 1993.

Omaha Star, The. "Most Blacks Shop Downtown." March 23, 1972.

---------------------. "Editorial: Workshop Good Move." October 28, 1993.

--------------------. "Impact Resolution Says 'Safety Major Concern'." November 5, 1981.

--------------------. "Minorities Obtain Record Amount of Business Loans." Vol. 41. No. 37. March 15, 1979.

--------------------. "News Conference Unveils New Hy-Vee Store." October 28, 1993.

--------------------. "24th Street Reopens as Two-Way Road on Nov. 28." December 2, 1993.

Omaha Sun, The. "Reevaluate North Freeway and Satisfy Both Sides." September 23, 1981.

Omaha World Herald, The. "Omahan Washington Says Black Voters Not Apathetic." March 17, 1980.

------------------------------------. "Economist Studies Highways' Effects." November 27, 1980.

------------------------------------. "North Omaha Gets New Loan Pool." September 16, 1993.

------------------------------------. "Group Begins Northeast Study." March 30, 1982.

------------------------------------. "Federal 'Partnerships' to Give Industries a Competitive Boost." January 2, 1994.

------------------------------------. "Planners Mold Future of Communities." December 19, 1993.

------------------------------------. "Urban League's Sound Message: Self-Help." January 24, 1994.

------------------------------------. "Apartment Complex Moves Step Closer to Renovation." October 22, 1980.

------------------------------------. "Omaha Freeway Called 'Poison'." September 16, 1981.

------------------------------------. "'Fulfill Obligation to North Omaha': Neighborhood Groups Pushing for Freeway." October 3, 1981.

------------------------------------. "North Omaha Sky Brightens." January 5, 1981.

Orlebeke, Charles J. "CDBG in Chicago: The Politics of Control." **Publius.** Vol. 13. No. 3. Summer 1983.

Page, Clarence. "Boston Chooses to Stay Intact." **The Chicago Tribune.** November 9, 1986.

Papajohn, George. "Richest, Poorest U.S. Suburbs? Right Here." **The Chicago Tribune.** March 29, 1987.

Parrott, Larry. "Eppley-Passenger Drop Tied to Economy." **Omaha World Herald.** January 18, 1982.

Peirce, Neal R. and Jerry Hagstrom. "Renewal, 1979 Style, in the South Bronx." **National Journal.** Vol. 40. October 6, 1979.

Poole, Marquita. "Taking Care of Our Own." **Essence.** September 1982.

Raspberry, William. "'Help' Did More to Hurt." **Omaha World Herald.** November 23, 1993.

Reilly, Mike. "90th Street, West Dodge Road Becomes Busiest Intersection." **Omaha World Herald.** November 26, 1993.

Roof, Wade C. (ed.) "Race and Residence in American Cities." **Annals of the American Academy of Political and Social Science.** January 1979.

Selby, Earl and Marian Selby. **Odyssey: Journey Through Black America.** New York: Putnam Publishing. 1971.

Stahl, David. "Landmark Settlement Reached." **Savings and Community Banker.** Vol. 3. Issue 1. January 1994.

Stelly, Matthew C. "Urban Planning or Social Planning?: North Omaha Being Divided and Decimated." **Omaha Star.** August 11, 1983.

-----------------------. "The Tavern License Process: An Examination of Hypocrisy." **The Milwaukee Courier.** August 4, 1990.

-----------------------. "Economic Development II: 'The Majkowski Syndrome' Revisited." **The Milwaukee Courier.** November 9, 1991.

-----------------------. "Economic Development III: Acquired Community Deficiency Syndrome." **The Milwaukee Courier.** November 16, 1991.

-----------------------. "The Norquist 'Vision' Revisited: An Assessment of His Promises." **The Milwaukee Courier**. September 23, 1989.

-----------------------. "Critic Cites Reasons for Opposition: Freeway Lacks Funds, Divides Blacks." **UNO Gateway**. February 19, 1982.

-----------------------. "'Minorities Could Help Build Omaha'." **Omaha World Herald**. June 7, 1982.

-----------------------. "'Fast Food Stamps': A Proposal to Help the Impoverished." **The Omaha Star**. June 16, 1983.

Stephens, George M. "Santa Cruz Cashes in on Downtown Revitalization." **Urban Land**. Vol. 38. No. 9. October 1979.

Straka, John W. "Boston Federal Reserve Study of Mortgage Discrimination." **Secondary Mortgage Markets.** Vol. 10. Issue 1. Winter 1993.

Strom, Fredric A., "Legal Standing of Citizen Groups." **Zoning and Planning Law** Report. Vol. 2. No. 11. October 1979.

Sullenberger, T. Earl and J. Harvey Kerns. **The Negro in Omaha: A Social Study of Negro Development.** Omaha, NE.: University of Omaha and Omaha Urban League. 1931.

Suzuki, Peter T. "Omaha's Black Vernacular--Cab Driver and His Fare: Facets of a Symbiotic Relationship." **The Western Journal of Black Studies.** Vol. 15. No. 2. 1991.

Taylor, John. "State to Pay OHA for Units Displaced by North Freeway." **Omaha World Herald.** May 15, 1981.

-----------------. "American National Puts Up $10 Million For North Omaha Loans." **The Omaha World Herald**. January 5, 1994.

Thomas, Fred. "Plan for Walgreen's on North 30th Criticized." **Omaha World Herald**. January 28, 1994.

Urban League of Nebraska. **The State of Black Omaha 1990.** Omaha, NE: Center for Applied Urban Research. 1990.

----------------------------------. **The State of Black Omaha 1984**. Omaha, NE: Center for Applied Urban Research. 1984.

----------------------------------. **The State of Black Omaha 1978**. Omaha, NE: Urban League of Nebraska. 1978.

Velasco, J.D. (2012, May 8). Cities face tough choices as federal funding for community programs dries up. *San Gabriel Valley Tribune.*

Wade, Richard. "America's Cities are (Mostly) Better than Ever." **American Heritage.** Vol. 30. No. 2. Febraury/March 1979.

Watson, Sheilah S. "Decentralizing Community Development: A Study of Oklahoma's Small Cities Program." **Publius.** Vol. 22. No. 1. Winter 1992.

Wilder, Marget G. **Black Assimilation in the Urban Environment: The Impact of Migration and Mobility**. Palo Alto, CA: R & E Research Associates, Inc. 1979.

Williams, J. Sherwood, B. Krishna Singh and Michael J. Miller. "Blacks and Southern Poverty." **Journal of Social and Behavioral** *Sciences.* Vol. 20. Winter 1974.

Witherspoon, Roger and S. Lee Hilliard. "No Trespassing!" **Black Enterprise.** May 1985.

Wilonsky, R. (2012, June 28). Are the arts centers worth the money? **Dallas Morning News.**

Wong, Charles Choy. "Black and Chinese Grocery Stores in Los Angeles Black Ghetto." **Urban Life.** Vol. 5. No. 4. January 1977.

Zerschling, Lynn. "Relocated Family Seeking Help on Repair Bill." **Omaha World Herald.** October 1, 1980.

----------------------. "Lower Home Values Vex North Omahans." **Omaha World Herald.** April 1980 (no specific date or page)

www.ingramcontent.com/pod-product-compliance
Lightning Source LLC
Chambersburg PA
CBHW081616250726
48657CB00009B/2594